Dictionary of
ENGLISH WORD-ROOTS

ENGLISH-ROOTS
AND ROOTS-ENGLISH

BY ROBERT W. L. SMITH

Dictionary of
ENGLISH
WORD-ROOTS

ENGLISH - ROOTS
and
ROOTS - ENGLISH

with examples and exercises

ROBERT W. L. SMITH

UNIVERSITY OF SANTA CLARA

1967

LITTLEFIELD, ADAMS & CO.
Totowa, New Jersey

INTRODUCTION

There are no long words in the English language. Even the example listed in this dictionary under "coni"—which, at forty-five letters is the longest word in Webster's Unabridged—is only a succession of shorter pieces, each of which has a simple meaning of its own.

This book is about those fragments of words, which may be called bases or elements and prefixes and suffixes, or may all be lumped together under the frightening appellation "segmental morphemes." I have chosen to call them simply word-roots because they are indeed the roots from which the English language grows.

If you are already familiar with word-roots, you will not be surprised at the way English words—even technical words which look long and difficult—explain themselves to you on the pages which follow. You may be surprised, though, to see a greater variety of roots and examples than you have seen in one place before. And I'm sure you'll be happy to find that the reversal of the dictionary—the English-to-roots section—makes possible a number of exercises which could not otherwise be used.

But if you are new to the workings of word-roots, you're in for a surprise and a treat as you discover that even the most complex of words consists of very simple parts which are anxious to tell you all about themselves.

Just to prove it, why not start with a look at that "coni" word? It looks absolutely monstrous, but a few minutes of flipping these pages should tell you that the roots say: "lung-beyond-small-looking-silicon-volcanic-dust-condition."

Without looking it up in a regular dictionary, you'll probably decide as I have that this horrendous collection of letters refers to "a lung condition caused by ultramicroscopic volcanic silicon dust" and is probably a miners' disease.

Although the word-roots listed here derive from many sources, the book offers no dry-as-dust inquiry into ancient languages long since dead, but a simple waking to awareness of the realities of living English. You can start by flipping the pages of the dictionary sections to see how common and technical words jostle each other for position as members of the same word-root families: *dexterity* and *dextrocardia, parent* and *oviparous, Nevada* and *nivicolous.* But sooner or later you'll want to move to the back of the book and face the prospect of filling the blanks that are waiting there to teach you.

In both sections I have tried to present the material simply and to stay out of the way of your work—and fun. Nevertheless, I have aimed at total accuracy in every detail and have regularly checked the material against the many authorities listed in the bibliography. I could not have taken greater care if I had written the book for myself alone, because originally I did. It gives me great pleasure to share it now with you. May it serve you well.

R. W. L. S.

University of Santa Clara
Santa Clara, California

for the one
who is well-named
"God's gracious gift"

Table of Contents

PART ONE
DICTIONARY

SECTION 1

Roots-to-English

A

-a	*feminine*	
	alumna Frederika Eugenia	
-a	*Greek plural ending*	
	phenomena criteria Lepidoptera	
a-	*in, on, at*	
	aboard aside asleep	
-a	*Latin ending*	
	formula lacuna scintilla	
-a	*Latin plural ending*	
	data agenda impedimenta	
a-, an-	*not, without*	
	atheist anarchy anonymous	
ab-	*away, from*	
	abnormal abduct abrasive	
ab-	see **ad-**	
-abad	*town, city*	
	Hyderabad Ahmadabad Saidabad	
abdomin	*abdomen*	
	abdominal abdominoscopy	
	abdominothoracic	
-able	*able to (be)*	
	portable curable tenable	

-ac, -iac	*related to*	
	maniac cardiac insomniac	
ac. acr	*sharp*	
	acute acrid acumen	
ac-	see **ad-**	
acanth	*thorn, spine*	
	acanthology acanthopod acanthoid	
acar	*mite*	
	acariasis acaroid acaricide	
-aceous	*having the quality of*	
	herbaceous saponaceous cretaceous	
acet	*vinegar*	
	acetic acetate acetometer	
acid	*sour, acid*	
	acidity acidosis acidulous	
acin	*grape*	
	acinose aciniform acinotubular	
-acious	*having the quality of*	
	tenacious loquacious vivacious	
-acity	*quality of*	
	veracity tenacity loquacity	
-acle	*that which*	
	receptacle tentacle spectacle	
acou, acu	*to hear*	
	acoustic acouesthesia osteoacusis	
acr	see **ac**	
acro	*high, extremity*	
	acrobat acrophobia acronym	
act	see **ag**	
actin	*ray*	
	actinic actinide actinomyces	
acu	see **acou**	
-acy, -cy	*state, quality, act*	
	infancy literacy accuracy	

-ad *group*
triad myriad decade

ad-, ab-, ac-, af-, *to, toward, against*
ag-, al-, an-, ap-, adhere advertise attend
as-, at-

adelph *brother*
Philadelphia adelphogamy adelphic

aden *gland*
adenoid adenitis adenectomy

adip *fat*
adipose adipocellular adiposuria

-ae *Latin plural ending*
alumnae nebulae antennae

aeg *goat*
aegis Aegopodium Aegocerus

aelur see **ailur**

aene *bronze, copper*
aeneous aeneolithic aeneomicans

aer *air*
aerate aerodynamics anaerobic

aesthes see **esthet**

aesthet see **esthet**

aeth *burnt, brown*
aethogen Aethionema Ethiopia

af- see **ad-**

aft *behind*
aft after abaft

ag- see **ad-**

ag, ig, act *to do, to drive*
agent ambiguous counteract

agap *love*
Agape Agapanthus Agapornis

agaric *fungus*
agaric agariciform agaricoid

agath	*good*	
	Agatha agathology Agathosma	
-age	*state, quality, act*	
	bondage courage portage	
agla	*bright*	
	aglaozonia Aglaspis Aglaonema	
agog	*leader*	
	pedagogue demagogue synagogue	
agon	*struggle*	
	agony protagonist antagonist	
agor	*marketplace*	
	agoraphobia allegory panegyric	
agr	*field*	
	agriculture agrarian agronomy	
agra	*seizure*	
	podagra agraphilydrus theragra	
ailur, aelur	*cat*	
	ailurophobia aelurophile Ailuropoda	
-air	see **-aire**	
-aire, -air	*one who, that which*	
	corsair millionaire questionnaire	
-al	*like, related to*	
	maternal pedal tactual	
al	*to nourish*	
	alimentary alimony *alma mater*	
al-	*the*	
	alcohol algebra alfalfa	
al-	see **ad-**	
al	see **alter**	
ala	*wing*	
	alate alar alisphenoid	
alam	*poplar*	
	alameda Alamo Los Alamos	
alb	*white*	
	album albino albumen	

alector, alectry	*cock*	
	alectoria alectryomachy alectryomancy	
alectry	see **alector**	
aleur	*flour*	
	aleurometer aleuronoid aleurone	
alex	*to protect*	
	Alexander alexin alexocyte	
alg	*pain*	
	neuralgia nostalgia analgesic	
all	*other*	
	allergy allegory allomorph	
allel	*mutually*	
	allelotropic allelomorph parallel	
alt	*high*	
	altitude altimeter altar	
alter, al	*other*	
	alternate alien altruist	
alum	*bitter*	
	alum aluminum aluminium	
alveol	*pit*	
	alveolar alveolo-labial alveus	
am	*to love*	
	amiable amorous amateur	
amar	*bitter*	
	amara amarine amaroid	
amaur	*dark*	
	amaurosis amaurotic amaurornis	
ambi-, amphi-	*both, around*	
	ambidextrous amphibious amphitheater	
ambly	*dull*	
	amblyacousia amblyopia amblychromasia	
ambul	*to walk*	
	ambulatory amble somnambulist	

americ	*America* americium Americomania Amerind
amni	*bowl, amnion* amniogenesis amnion amniotic
amoeb	*change, amoeba* amoeba amoeboid amoebocyte
amphi-	see **ambi-**
ampull	*flask* ampulla ampulliform Ampullaria
amygdal	*almond, tonsil* amygdalectomy amygdaloid amygdalase
amyl	*starch* amylosynthesis amylase amyloclast
-an	*like, related to* urban agrarian American
-an, -ian	*one who* artisan magician optician
an	*ring, anus* anal anoscopy ano-coccygeal
an-	see **a-**
an-	see **ad-**
an-	see **ana-**
-ana	*information about* Americana Jeffersoniana Californiana
ana-	*up, back, again* anatomy analysis anchronism
anatol	*east* anatolian Anatole Anatola
-ance	*state, quality, act* dominance radiance resistance
-ancy	*state, quality, act* constancy buoyancy hesitancy
ancyl	see **ankyl**

-and	see **-end**
andr	*man* polyandry Andrew gynandromorph
-ane	*like, related to* urbane mundane humane
-aneity, -eity	*quality* simultaneity contemporaneity heterogeneity
anem	*wind* anemology anemometer anemography
-aneous	*having the quality of* instantaneous contemporaneous simultaneous
angel	*message, messenger, angel* angel evangelist angelica
angi	*vessel, blood vessel* angiograph angiectomy sporangiferous
angl	*English* Anglican Anglophobe Anglo-Saxon
angl	see **angul**
angui	*snake* anguiform anguiped Anguilla
angul, angl	*angle* triangle angulometer anguliferous
angust	*narrow* angustifoliate anguish Angostura
anima	*spirit* animal inanimate equanimity
ankyl, ancyl	*crooked* ankylosis ankylodactylia ancylostomiasis
ann, enn	*year* annual anniversary centennial
annel, annul	*ring* annular anneloid Annelida

annul	see **annel**
ans	*handle* ansate ansiform ansotomy
anser	*goose* anserine anseriform anserous
-ant	*one who, that which, -ing* participant pendant secant
ant-	see **anti-**
ante-	*before* anteroom antecedent antediluvian
anter-	*front, before* anterior anterodorsal anterospinal
anth	*flower* anther chrysanthemum anthology
anthrac	*coal, carbuncle* anthracite anthracoid anthrax
anthrop	*man, human being* anthropology philanthropist anthropomorphic
anti-, ant-	*against, opposite* antisocial antiseptic antithesis
antr	*cavern, sinus* antrum antroscope antrodynia
aort	*to lift, to hang* aorta aortic aortopathy
ap-	see **ad-**
ap-	see **apo-**
apert	*to open* aperture aperitif April
aph	see **hapt**
aphr	*foam* aphrolite aphrite Aphrodite
aphrodis	*Aphrodite (goddess)* aphrodisiac aphrodisia aphrodisiomania

api	*bee* apiary apian apiculture
apic	*top, extremity* apex apical apico-alveolar
apo-, ap-	*away, from* apogee apostle apheter
-apse	see **hapt**
apt, ept	*to adjust, to fit* aptitude adapt inept
aqua	*water* aquarium aquamarine aqueduct
aquil	*eagle* aquiline aquila eagle
-ar	*like, related to* circular ocular regular
-ar	*one who* liar beggar bursar
arachn	*spider* arachnid arachnoid arachnodactyly
arc	*bow, arc* arciform arcograph arcosolium
arch	*first, to rule* archenemy monarch anarchy
arct	*north, bear (animal)* Arctic Antarctic Arcteranthis
arct	*to press together* arctation coarctate aortarctia
-ard, -art	*one who (pejorative)* drunkard coward braggart
-ard	see **hard**
are	*space* area areola aerie
aren	*sand* arena arenicolous arenaceous

areo	*Mars (Ares)* areography areocentric Areopagus
argent	*silver* Argentina argentiferous argentaffin
argyr	*silver* hydrargyrum miargyrite argyrocephalous
arid	*dry, to burn* arid ardent arson
arithm	*number* arithmetic logarithm arithmomania
-arium	see **-ary**
arm	*arm, weapon* army armament alarm
arsen	*manly, arsenic* arsenious arsenotherapy Arsenoxenus
art	*art, skill, craft* artisan artifact artificial
-art	see **-ard**
art	see **arthr**
arter	*artery* arterial arteriosclerosis periarteritis
arthr, art	*joint* arthritis arthropod article
-ary	*like, related to* sedentary sanitary temporary
-ary	*one who* revolutionary reactionary lapidary
-ary, -arium	*place where* mortuary granary planetarium
as-	see **ad-**
asc	*bag* ascocarp ascospore ascidiform
ascid	see **asc**

-asia, -asis	*state, quality, act* euthanasia antonomasia metasomasis
asin	*jackass* asinine asininity easel
-asis	see **-asia**
-asm	*state, quality, act* sarcasm enthusiasm pleonasm
asper	*rough* asperity exasperate asperate
aspid	*shield* aspidate Aspidobranchia Aglaspis
-ast	*one who* enthusiast pederast scholiast
-aster	*inferior* poetaster criticaster oleaster
aster, astr	*star* asterisk astronaut disaster
asthm	*breathless* asthma asthmatic asthmogenic
astr	see **aster**
astragal	*ankle-bone* astragalus astragalectomy astragalotibial
at-	see **ad-**
-ate	*to make, to act* captivate dehydrate saturate
-ate	*one who, that which* advocate delegate aggregate
-ate	*having the quality of* literate affectionate passionate
athen	*Athena (goddess)* Athens athenaeum attic
ather	*gruel, fat* atheroma atherogenic atherosclerosis
athl	*contest, prize* athlete pentathlon decathlon

| **-atim** | *in the manner of* |
| | verbatim   seriatim   guttatim |

| **atlant** | *Atlas (the Titan)* |
| | Atlantic   Atlantis   atlas |

| **atm** | *breath* |
| | atmosphere   atmometer   atmophile |

| **atr** | *black* |
| | atrocious   atrocity   atrabilious |

| **atri** | *atrium* |
| | atrial   sino-atrial   atriopore |

| **audi** | *to hear* |
| | audience   auditorium   inaudible |

| **aug** | *to increase* |
| | augment   auction   author |

| **augur** | *soothsayer* |
| | augur   augury   inauguration |

| **aul** | *flute, pipe* |
| | hydraulic   aulophyte   Aulostoma |

| **aur** | *air, breeze* |
| | aura   aurophore   soar |

| **aur** | *ear* |
| | auricular   binaural   auscultation |

| **aur** | *gold* |
| | auriferous   aureole   aureate |

| **austral** | *south* |
| | Australia   australorbis   australopithecus |

| **auto-** | *self* |
| | automobile   autograph   autonomous |

| **aux** | *increase* |
| | auxiliary   auxocyte   enterauxe |

| **av** | *to desire* |
| | avid   avarice   avaricious |

| **avi** | *bird* |
| | aviary   aviator   aviculture |

ax, axon	*axis*
	axilla axofugal axonometer
axon	see **ax**

B

bacc	*berry*
	bacciferous bacciform baccivorous
bacch	*Bacchus (god)*
	bacchanal bacchanalian bacchic
bacill	*bacillus, small staff*
	bacilliform bacillophobia bacillemia
back	*back*
	backward aback bacon
bacter	*small staff*
	bacterium bactericidal bacteriophage
bak	*to bake*
	bakery batch Baxter
balaen	*whale*
	balaenoid Balaena Balaenoptera
balan	*acorn, gland, penis*
	balanophore balanitis Balanops
ball	*ball*
	balloon ballot bullet
ball	see **bol**
ban	*to proclaim, to banish*
	banns contraband bandit
bane	*death*
	bane baneful henbane
bank	*bench*
	bank bankrupt banquet
bapt	*to dip*
	baptize baptism pedobaptism

bar	*pressure, weight* barometer barograph isobar
bar-	*son of* Bartholomew *Bar Mitzvah* Bar-Jona
barbar	*stranger, foreign* barbarian barbarism Barbara
barr	*board, obstruction* barrier barricade barrister
bas, bat, bet	*to go, to walk* abasia acrobat diabetes
basi	*bottom* basilar basiplast basi-occipital
basil	*king, royal* basilica Basil basilisk
bass	*low* bass basset bassoon
bat	*to strike* combat batter debate
bat	see **bas**
bath	*deep* bathyscaphe bathysphere bathos
be-	*intensive, to make* bedeck bemuse bewhiskered
bead	see **bid**
beck	*sign* beck beckon beacon
bel	*bag, to swell* belly bellows Belgium
bell	*beautiful* belle belladonna embellish
bell	*war* belligerent bellicose rebellion
ben-	*son of* Benjamin Ben-Hur Ben-Gurion

| **bene-** | *good, well* |
| | benefactor benevolent benediction |

| **bengal** | *Bengal (India)* |
| | Bengalese Bengali bungalow |

| **ber** | *to carry, to bear* |
| | bear birth bier |

| **-berg** | *mountain* |
| | iceberg Heidelberg Nuremberg |

| **bert** | *bright* |
| | Robert Albert Bertha |

| **bet** | see **bas** |

| **bi-** | *two* |
| | bicycle biped bigamy |

| **bib** | *to drink* |
| | imbibe bib bibulous |

| **bibli** | *book* |
| | bibliophile bibliography Bible |

| **bid, bead** | *to ask, to pray* |
| | bid forbid bead |

| **bide** | *to stay* |
| | bide abide abode |

| **bil** | *bile* |
| | bilious bilirubin biliverdin |

| **bind** | *to bind* |
| | bind band bond |

| **bio** | *life* |
| | biology autobiography antibiotic |

| **blanc** | *white, pale* |
| | blanch blank *carte blanche* |

| **blast** | *to sprout, bud* |
| | blastula blastogenesis odontoblast |

| **blaw** | *to blow, to swell* |
| | blow bladder blast |

| **blaz** | *torch* |
| | blaze blazer emblazon |

bleach	*white, pale* bleach bleachers bleak
bled, blod	*blood* bleed bloody bless
blenn	*mucus* blennogenous blenniform balanoblennorrhea
blep	*to look, to see* ablepsia ablepsy hemiablepsia
blephar	*eyelid, cilium* blepharitis blepharoncus blepharoplast
bol, ball	*to throw* hyperbole metabolism embolism
bomb	*dull noise* bomb bombard boom
bon	*good* bonny *bon vivant* boon
bor	*farmer, peasant* neighbor boorish Boer
bord	*board* boarder border starboard
boreal	*north* boreal borealization *aurora borealis*
-borough	see **-bury**
bosc, bot	*to graze, plant* proboscis botany botanophile
botul	*sausage* botulism botuliferous botuliform
bou, bov	*cow, ox* bovine bucolic bugle
bov	see **bou**
bow	*to bend* bow elbow buxom
brac	*arm* bracelet embrace brace

brachi *arm*
brachiate brachial brachiopod

brachy- *short*
brachymorphic brachycephalic
brachycardia

brad *broad, wide*
broad breadth Bradley

brady- *slow*
bradykinetic bradycardia bradylogia

bran see **burn**

branchi *gill, fin*
branchia branchiopod Nudibranchia

brek *to break*
breaker broken brick

brest *breast*
abreast breastplate brisket

brev *short*
brevity abbreviate breviary

brew *to ferment*
brewery Brewster bread

-bridge, -bruck *bridge*
Cambridge Stourbridge Innsbruck

broc *to stitch, to pierce, to tap (keg)*
brocade broach broker

brom *stench*
bromine bromide podobromidrosis

bronch *windpipe*
bronchial bronchitis bronchoscope

bront *thunder*
brontosaur brontophobia brontometer

-bruck see **-bridge**

brun *brown*
brunette bruin brunish

-brunn see **-burn**

| **bry** | *moss, to swell* |
| | bryology   bryophyte   embryo |

| **bucc** | *cheek, mouth* |
| | buccal   buccolabial   buccilingual |

| **bul** | *to will* |
| | abulia   hyperbulia   bulesis |

| **bulg** | *bag* |
| | bulge   budget   budgetary |

| **bull** | *bubble, seal* |
| | ebullient   boil   bulletin |

| **-bund, -bond** | *tending toward* |
| | moribund   pudibund   vagabond |

| **-burg, -burgh** | *fort, town* |
| | Hamburg   Pittsburgh   Edinburgh |

| **burg** | *shelter, town* |
| | burgess   burglar   burrow |

| **-burgh** | see **-burg** |

| **burn, bran** | *to burn* |
| | burn   brand   brandy |

| **-burn, -brunn** | *spring* |
| | Bannockburn   Blackburn   Schoenbrunn |

| **burs** | *bag, sack* |
| | bursitis   disburse   reimburse |

| **-bury, -borough** | *fort, town* |
| | Canterbury   Salisbury   Peterborough |

| **butyr** | *butter* |
| | butyric   butyrin   butyrometer |

| **-by** | *town* |
| | Derby   Whitby   Grimsby |

| **byss, byth** | *bottom, depth* |
| | abyss   abysmal   Bythites |

| **byss** | *linen, flax* |
| | byssus   byssiferous   byssinosis |

| **byth** | see **byss** |

C

cac *bad*
cacophony   cacogenics   arthrocace

cad, cid, cas *to fall, to happen*
decadent   coincidence   casualty

cadm *Kadmos (Greek hero)*
cadmia   cadmium   calamine

caduc *falling*
caducibranch   caducicorn   ʾcaducous

caec, cec *blind*
caecum   cecitis   caecostomy

caen see **cen**

caes, ces *blue*
caesium   cesium   caesious

caesar *(Julius) Caesar*
caesarean   czar   Jersey

cal *hot*
calorie   caldron   calescent

calam *reed*
calamiferous   Calamites   Calamospermae

calc *heel*
recalcitrant   calcaneus   inculcate

calc *lime*
calcium   calculate   chalk

calce *shoe*
discalced   calceiform   Calceolaria

calcul *pebble*
calculate   calculus   calculiform

calli *beautiful*
calligraphy   calisthenics   calliope

calyc *cup, bell*
calyciflorous   calyx   chalice

calypt *hidden, covered*
calyptoblastic   eucalyptus   calypter

camer	*chamber* camera chamber comrade
camp	*field* campaign encampment champagne
campan	*bell* campanile campanology campaniform
campt	*curved* camptodrome Camptosorus camptosaur
campyl	*curved* campylodrome campylotropous campylognathia
can, cyn	*dog* canine canary cynic
can, con, ken	*to know (how)* can conning keen
can	*reed, tube, hollow* cannon canyon cane
can	*rod, rule* canon law canonical canonize
canal	*canal* canal canaliculus channel
cancel	*crossbar, lattice* cancellation chancellor chancery
cancer, chancr	*crab, cancer* cancer cancrology chancre
cand	*white, glowing* incandescent candid candle
cani	*gray* canities canitist caniceps
cant	*song* incantation canticle recant
cap	*cape* cap escape chapel
cap, cip, cept, ceive	*to take* capture intercept deceive

capill	*hair*
	capillary capilliform Capillaria
capit	*head*
	capital decapitate recapitulate
capn	*smoke*
	capnomancy hypercapnia Capnodium
capr	*goat*
	caper capricorn Capri
caps	*container, box*
	capsule encapsulate casket
car	*dear*
	caress charitable cherish
car	*vehicle*
	car chariot carriage
carbo	*coal, charcoal*
	carbon carbohydrate carbonuria
carcin	*crab, cancer*
	carcinoma carcinosis carcinectomy
card	*heart*
	cardiac pericardium endocarditis
cari	*decay*
	caries carious carrion
carl	*man, freeman*
	churlish Carl Charles
carn	*flesh, meat*
	carnal incarnate carnivorous
carotid	*stupor*
	carotid carotic caroticotympanic
carp	*fruit*
	carpology polycarpous carpophagous
carp	*wrist*
	carpus carpal metacarpal
carph	*straw*
	carpholite carphology carphosiderite

cart	*paper, card*
	card chart cartoon
cartilag	*gristle*
	cartilage cartilaginous cartilaginoid
caryo-	see **karyo-**
cas	*house*
	casino Casablanca cassock
case	*cheese*
	caseate casease casein
cast	*pure*
	caste castigate incest
-caster, -cester	*camp, fort*
	Lancaster Manchester Winchester
cat	*cat*
	tomcat caterpillar caterwaul
cat-	see **cata-**
cata-, cath-, cat-	*down, away, thoroughly*
	catastrophe catalogue catholic
caten	*chain*
	concatenate concatenation chain
cath, kath	*pure*
	catharsis cathartic Katharine
cath-	see **cata-**
caud	*tail*
	caudal coward cue
caul	*stalk*
	cauliform cauliflorous caulotaxy
caust, caut	*to burn*
	caustic holocaust cauterize
caut	see **caust**
cav	*hollow*
	cave concave excavate
caval	*horse*
	cavalry cavalcade chivalry

cec	see **caec**
cede, ceed, cess	*to go, to yield* recede proceed secession
ceed	see **cede**
ceive	see **cap**
cel	*heaven, sky* celestial Celeste ceiling
cel	see **-cele**
cel	see **coel**
-cele, cel	*tumor, hernia* gastrocele celectomy hydrocele
celer	*fast* celerity accelerate decelerate
cell	*to hide* cell cellar conceal
cell	*room, cell* cellular celliferous celliform
cen	*empty* cenotaph cenophobia cenanthous
cen, caen, -cene	*new, recent* cenogenesis caenopithecus Eocene
cen, coen	*common* cenobite coenesthesia coenoblast
-cene	see **cen**
cens	*to assess* censor censure census
cent	*hundred* century centipede centigrade
cente	*puncture* centesis cephalocentesis pneumonocentesis
centr	*center* concentric concentration centrifugal

cephal	*head*
	cephalic encephalitis brachycephalic
cept	see **cap**
cer	*wax*
	cerecloth ceroplastics ceromel
cerat	see **kerat**
ceraun, keraun	*lightning*
	ceraunograph ceraunophone
	keraunophobia
cerc	*tail*
	cercus homocercal cercopithecus
cere	*Ceres (goddess)*
	cereal cerium Ceres (asteroid)
cerebr	*cerebrum, brain*
	cerebral cerebration cerebrospinal
cern, cert	*to perceive, to make certain*
	discern ascertain certificate
cert	see **cern**
cerule	*blue*
	cerulean ceruleite cerulignol
cervic	*neck*
	cervix cervical cervicofacial
ces	see **caes**
cess	see **cede**
cest	*girdle*
	cestodiasis Cestoda Polycesta
-cester	see **-caster**
cet	*whale*
	cetology cetacean ceticide
chaet, chet	*bristle*
	chaetognath chaeta spirochete
chalaz	*hailstone, lump*
	chalazion chalaza chalazodermia

chalc   *copper, bronze*
                 chalcocite   leucochalcite   chalcolithic

chamae   *low, earth*
                 chameleon   chamaecephalic   chamomile

chancr   see **cancer**

charg   *to load*
                 charge   discharge   cargo

charis   *favor, gratitude*
                 eucharist   eucharistic   charisma

chasm   *opening*
                 chasmogamy   chasmophyte
                 chasmatoplasm

cheap   *to buy*
                 cheap   cheapen   Chapman

cheil, chil   *lip*
                 cheiloschisis   Chilopsis   Cheilostomata

cheir   see **chir**

chel   *hoof, claw*
                 chelate   chelophore   chelicera

chem   *to pour*
                 chemistry   alchemy   chemotropism

chen   *goose*
                 chenopod   Cheniscus   Chenendroscyphia

chet   see **chaet**

chias   *chi-shaped (X)*
                 chiasmus   chiastolite   chiastoneural

chil   see **cheil**

chil   see **col**

chili-   see **kilo-**

chio   see **chion**

chion, chio   *snow*
                 chionanthus   chionablepsia   chiolite

chir, cheir   *hand*
                 chiropractor   chiropodist   macrocheiria

chlor	*green*
	chlorine chlorophyll chlorosis
choan	*funnel*
	choana choanocyte choanosome
chol	*bile, gall*
	choleric melancholy cholera
chondr	*grain, cartilage*
	chondroma chondrectomy mitochondrion
chor	*area*
	chorepiscopus chorology chorography
chor	*to dance*
	chorus choreography chorea
chord	*string*
	chordate notochord Chordata
chori	*fetal membrane, skin*
	endochorion chorioretinal choroid
chorist	*separated*
	choristate choristoblastoma choristoma
chres	*use*
	catachresis chrestomathy chreotechnics
christ	*Christ, anointed*
	christen criss-cross cretin
chrom, chro	*color*
	chromosome achromatic panchromatic
chron	*time*
	chronic chronometer chronicle
chrys	*gold, yellow*
	chrysanthemum chrysalis chrysolite
chthon	*earth*
	autochthonous chthonophagia chthonian
chyl	*fluid, juice*
	chyliferous hypochylia chylocyst
chym	*fluid, juice*
	chymiferous chymogen parenchymous
cid	see **cad**

-cide, cis	*to kill, to cut* fratricide genocide incision
cili	*eyelash, eyelid* cilium ciliary supercilious
cimic	*bedbug* cimex cimicide cimicoid
cinct	*to bind* precinct succinct cincture
cinema-	see **kine-**
ciner	*ash* incinerator cinereous cinerarium
cion	*pillar, uvula* cionitis cionectomy cionocranial
cip	see **cap**
circul	*round* circular circulus circellus
circum-	*around* circumstance circumference circumnavigate
cirr, cirrh	*curl* cirrus cirriped cirrhitidae
cirr, cirrh	*yellow* cirrhosis cirrhotic cirrolite
cirrh	see **cirr**
cis-, citra-	*on this side* cisapline cis-Alleghany citramontane
cis	see **-cide**
cit	*to summon, to impel* citation incite excitement
citr	*citrus* citric citronella citron
citra-	see **cis-**
civ	*citizen* civil civilian civilization

clad	*sprout*
	cladophyll acanthocladous cladanthous
claim	see **clam**
clam	*bond, to stick*
	clam clamber climb
clam, claim	*to shout*
	clamor proclamation exclaim
clar	*clear*
	declare clarify clarity
clas	*to break*
	iconoclast cranioclast clinoclase
claud	*lame*
	claudication Claude Gladys
claus	see **clud**
clav	*club*
	claviform clavicorn Claviceps
clav	*key*
	conclave clavicle clavichord
clav	*nail*
	clavus clavellated clavelization
clavic	*clavicle*
	clavicula clavicular clavicotomy
-cle, -cule	*small*
	particle corpuscle molecule
clean	*clean*
	cleanse cleanly unclean
cleav	*to split*
	cleaver cleavage cleft
cleav	*to stick*
	cleave cliff clay
cleid, cleis	*key, clavicle*
	cleidocranial cleidomancy enterocleisis
cleis	see **cleid**

cler	*lot, portion* clergy cleric clerk
climac	*ladder* climacteric climax climacium
climat	see **clin**
clin, climat	*to lean, slope* recline clinic climate
cloac	*sewer* cloaca Cloacina Cloacitrema
clon	*spasm* clonus clonic clonicotonic
close	see **clud**
cloth	*cloth* clothing clothes clad
clud, clus, **claus, close**	*to close* include exclusive clause
clus	see **clud**
clype	*shield* clypeus clypeate clypeofrontal
cnem	*shinbone, tibia* cnemitis cnemoscoliosis platycnemic
cnid	*nettle* cnidoblast cnidocil cnidosis
co-	see **com-**
cobalt	*devil, cobalt* cobaltic cobaltiferous cobaltocyanic
cocc	*berry, spherical bacterium* coccigenic streptococcus staphylococcus
coccyg	*cuckoo* coccyx coccygeal coccygectomy
cochl	*shell, spoon* cochleate cochleariform cochlear
coct	*to cook* concoction decoct precocious

coel, cel	*hollow* coelenterate blastocoel hydrocoele
coeli	*belly* coeliotomy coelialgia coelioscopy
coen	see **cen**
cogn	*to know* recognize incognito connoisseur
cohort	*enclosure, garden* court cohort courtier
coin	see **cen**
col, chil	*cold* cold cool chilly
col	*to filter* percolate colander culvert
col	*large intestine* colon colic colonic
col, cult	*to till, to inhabit* colony cultivation culture
col-	see **com-**
cole	*sheath* coleus coleopteron coleorhiza
coll	*glue* collage colloid protocol
coll	*neck* collar decollete collopexia
color	*color* tricolor discolor coloratura
colp	*hollow, vagina* endocolpitis colposcope colpidium
colubr	*snake* colubrine Colubrina Coluber
columb	*dove, pigeon* columbine columbarium Columbiformes

com	*hair*
	comephorous comoid comet
com	*a revel*
	encomium comedy encomiastic
com	*to sleep*
	coma comatose cemetery
com-, co-, col-, con-, cor-	*with, together, intensive*
	compress contemporary cooperate
combur	*to burn up*
	comburimeter combustion comburivorous
come	*to come*
	income outcome welcome
comit	*companion*
	concomitant count (noble) constable
con	*cone*
	coniform conifer conical
con	see **can**
con-	see **com-**
conch	*shell*
	conch conchiform conchitic
cond	*to hide*
	abscond recondite Escondido
condyl	*knuckle*
	condyle condyloma condylura
coni, koni	*dust*
	pneumonoultramicroscopicsilicovol-canoconiosis
contra-, counter-	*against, opposite*
	contradict contrary counterspy
cop	*to cut*
	syncopate syncope apocopate
copi	*abundance*
	copious copy cornucopia

copr	*dung*
	coproma coprolith coprolalia
copul	*bond*
	copula copulative couple
cor	*doll, pupil (of eye)*
	isocoria coroplasty coreometer
cor	*leather*
	excoriate scourge cuirass
cor-	see **com-**
corac	*raven*
	coracidium coracite coracoid
corall	*coral*
	coralliform coralloid Corallorhiza
cord	*heart*
	cordial record concord
corn	*horn*
	unicorn cornucopia Capricorn
coron	*wreath, crown*
	coronation coronet coroner
corp	*body*
	corpse incorporate corpulent
cortic	*bark, rind*
	corticosterone corticifugal corticospinal
coryn	*club*
	Corynebacterium Corynomorpha Leucocoryne
cosm	*universe, harmony*
	cosmic cosmonaut microcosm
cosmet	*beauty, harmony*
	cosmetic cosmesis cosmetology
cost	*rib, side, coast*
	costal accost cutlet
cotyl	*cup*
	dicotylous cotyloid Cotylophora

counter-	see **contra-**
coup	*to cut, to strike* coupon coupe cope
course	see **cur**
cover	*to cover, to hide* covert discover curfew
cox	*hip* coxa coxosternal coxalgia
crac	see **crat**
crak	*to crack* crack crackle crash
crani	*skull* cranium pericranium intracranial
cras	*mixing* idiosyncrasy crasis Craseomys
-crat, crac	*to rule* democrat aristocracy Hippocrates
cre-	see **creat**
creat	*to make* creative creature recreation
creat, cre-, kre-	*meat, flesh* pancreas creosote kreotoxism
cred	*to believe* credible credit credential
crek	*to croak* creak croak cricket (insect)
crepit	*to crackle, to crack* crepitation decrepit decrepitude
cresc, crease, cret, cru	*to grow* crescendo increase accretion
cret	*chalk* cretaceous cretify cretification
cri	*to judge* criticize criterion crisis

cri	*a ram*	
	criophore crioboly criosphinx	
cric	*ring*	
	cricothyroid cricoid cricotomy	
crimin	*charge, crime*	
	criminal incriminate recrimination	
crin	*hair*	
	criniculture crinigerous crinoline	
crin	*lily*	
	crinoid crinum Actinocrinus	
crin	*to separate*	
	endocrine crinogenic crisis	
croc	*hook, bend*	
	crochet crouch crotch	
cruc	*cross*	
	crucifix crusade cruise	
crur	*shank, leg*	
	crural crurotarsal Crurosaurus	
crust	*hard covering*	
	crust encrusted crustacean	
cry, kry	*cold*	
	cryogen cryotherapy kryokonite	
crym	*frost, cold*	
	crymotherapy crymodynia	
	crymo-anesthesia	
crypt, krypt	*hidden*	
	crypt cryptic krypton	
cryst	*crystal*	
	crystallography phenocryst	
	crystalliferous	
cten	*comb*	
	ctenoid ctenophore Ctenidae	
cub	see **cumb**	
-cule	see **-cle**	

culp	*fault, blame* culprit culpable exculpate
cult	see **col**
cumb, cub	*to lie (down)* succumb incumbent incubator
cumber	*to obstruct* cumbersome encumber encumbrance
cumul	*heap* accumulate cumulative cumulus
-cund, -und	*like, related to* rubicund jocund rotund
cune	*wedge* cuneiform cuneate cuneonavicular
cup	*to desire* cupidity concupiscence Cupid
cupr	*copper* cuprite cupreous cupric
cur	*care* pedicure curator sinecure
cur, course	*to run* current concourse recur
curv	*curved* curvature curviform curvilinear
cuspid	*point* cuspid bicuspid cuspidate
cuss	*to strike* concussion percussion repercussion
custod	*guard* custody custodian custodial
cut	*skin* cuticle cutaneous subcutaneous
cutl	*knife* cutlass cutlery cutler
-cy	see **-acy**

cyan	*blue* cyanide cyanosis cyanoderma
cyath	*cup* cyathiform cyathozooid cyatholith
cycl	*circle* tricycle cyclone Cyclops
cym	see **kym**
cymb	*boat, bowl* cymbal cymbocephalic Cymbidium
cyn	see **can**
cypr	*Cyprus* Cypriot Cypro-Turkish copper
cyst	*bladder* cyst cystoscope nephrocystitis
cyt	*cell* cytology cytogenesis leucocyte

D

dacry	*tear (-drop)* dacrcyocyst dacryoma dacryocystitis
dactyl	*finger* dactylic pterodactyl date (fruit)
dal, tal	*valley* dale taler dollar
dam	*woman, lady* dame madam damsel
damn	*loss* damnation condemn indemnity
das	*dense* dasymeter dasyure Dasiphora
dat	see **don**
day	*day* daylight daisy dawn

de-	*away, down, negative*
	decapitate deciduous demerit
deal	*part*
	dealer ordeal dole
dear	*precious*
	dearth darling endearing
deb	*to owe*
	debt debit debenture
dec	*becoming (proper)*
	decent decorate indecorous
dec, deka	*ten*
	decimal December decimate
dei, div	*God*
	deity deify divine
dein	see **din**
deipn	*dinner*
	deipnosophist deipnophobia
	Deipnopsocus
deka	see **dec**
del	*to destroy*
	delete deletion indelible
delph	*dolphin*
	dephinium delphocurarine
	Delphinapterus
delt	*delta-shaped ($\triangle$)*
	delta deltaic deltoid
dem	*to judge*
	deem doom doomsday
dem	see **des**
demi-	*half*
	demigod demitasse demivolt
demo	*people*
	democracy epidemic demagogue
demon	*demon*
	pandemonium demonology demonolatry

dendr	*tree* dendrology philodendron rhododendron
dent	*tooth* dentist dentifrice dandelion
derm	*skin* dermatology epidermis hypodermic
des, dem	*bond, ligament* diadem arthrodesis desmopexy
desider	*to want* desideratum desire desirable
deuter	*second* deuterium deuterogenesis Deuteronomy
dextr	*right hand* ambidextrous dexterity dextrocardia
di-	*two* diphthong dioxide dichromatic
di-	see **dia-**
di-	see **dis-**
dia	*day* diary dial dismal
dia-, di-	*through, between* diameter diagonal dialogue
diabol	*devil* diabolical diabolism devil
dich-	*two* dichotomy dichoptic dichogamy
dict	*to speak* predict verdict malediction
dicty, dikty	*net* dictyogen dictyosome diktyonite
didym	*twin* didymolite neodymium gastrodidymus
dif-	see **dis-**

dig   *to excavate*
      dig   dike   ditch

digit   *finger, toe*
      digit   digital   digitalis

dign   *worthy*
      dignity   dignitary   condign

dikty   see **dicty**

din, dein   *terrible*
      dinosaur   Dinotherium   Deinodon

din   *whirling*
      Dinobryon   Dinoflagellata   Melodinus

diplo-   *double*
      diploma   diplopia   diplococcus

dips   *thirst*
      dipsomania   dipsotherapy   Dipsosaurus

dis-, di-, dif-   *away, negative*
      dismiss   differ   disallow

disc   *disk*
      discus   discomycete   dish

div   see **dei**

doc   *to teach*
      doctor   doctrine   docile

dodeca-   *twelve*
      dodecahedron   dodecasyllable
      dodecaphonic

dog, dox   *opinion, praise*
      dogma   orthodox   doxology

dol   *grief*
      doleful   condolence   Dolores

dolicho-   *long*
      dolichocephalic   dolichomorphic
      dolichosaurus

dom   *home*
      domestic   domicile   majordomo

-dom	*state, quality*
	serfdom kingdom wisdom
domin	*master*
	dominate domineer dominion
don	*to do*
	done do deed
don, dat	*to give*
	donation condone data
dor	*gift*
	Theodore Dorothy Pandora
-dorf, -thorpe	*town*
	Düsseldorf Althorp Linthorpe
dorm	*to sleep*
	dormant dormitory dormouse
dors	*back (of body)*
	dorsal endorse dorsispinal
dos, dot	*to give*
	dose antidote anecdote
dox	see **dog**
dra	*to do*
	drama dramatic drastic
drag	*to draw*
	drag draw draft
drif	*to drive*
	drift adrift drive
drink	*to drink*
	drinker drunk drown
drip	*to drip*
	dripping drop dribble
drom	*to run, course*
	syndrome hippodrome hemodrometer
dryg	*dry*
	dry drug drought
du-	*two*
	dual duplex duplicate

duc	*to lead*
	produce abduct duchess
dulc	*sweet*
	dulcet dulcimer douceur
duodec-,	*twelve*
duoden-	duodecimal duodenary duodenum
duoden-	see **duodec-**
dur	*hard, lasting*
	durable obdurate enduring
dy-	*two*
	dyarchy dyad dyotheism
dyn, dynam	*power*
	dynamite dynasty thermodynamics
dynam	see **dyn**
dys-	*bad, badly*
	dystrophy dysentery dysplastic
dysi	*clothing*
	ecdysis ecdysiast endysis

E

e-, ex-	*out, away*
	emit expulsion exhale
eburn	*ivory*
	eburnean eburnation eburnated
ec-	*out, away*
	eccentric ecstasy ectopic
eccles	*church*
	ecclesiastical ecclesiarch ecclesiology
ech	*sound*
	echo catechumen catechism
ech	see **hec**
echin	*spiny*
	echinoderm echinosis Echinomastus

eco-, oec	*home* economy ecumenical androecium
ecto-	*outer, outside* ectoderm ectomorphic ectoplasm
edaph	*bottom, ground* edaphic edaphology edaphosauria
edema	*to swell* edema edematous edematigenous
-ee	*one who (passive)* divorcee employee payee
-eer	*one who* volunteer mutineer auctioneer
ef-	see **e-**
ego	*I, self* egotist egocentric *alter ego*
eid	see **id**
eido	*resemblance, form* eidoptometry Eidotheca Eidothrips
-eity	see **-aneity**
-ek, -ik	*descendant of, little* Adamek Gromek Lukasik
-el	*little, small* parcel novel cerebellum
elaph	*deer* elaphomyces elaphodus elaphoglossum
elaphr	*light (in weight)* Elaphrium Elaphrocnemus Elaphrus
elasm	*metal plate* elasmobranch elasmothere elasmosaur
electr	*electric, amber* electricity electrode electrolysis
eleuther	*free* eleutheromania eleutheropetalous Eleutherodactylus

-em	*something done*	system theorem stratagem
em-	see **en-**	
em	see **hem**	
-eme	*something done*	grapheme morpheme phoneme
emet	*to vomit*	emetic emesis emetatrophia
empt	*to buy, to take*	exempt redemption example
en-, em-	*in, into, intensive*	enclose parenthesis enliven
-en	*to make*	weaken harden loosen
-en	*having the quality of*	wooden rotten woolen
-ence	*state, quality, act*	dependence residence competence
encephal	*brain*	encephalitis encephalography metencephalon
-ency	*state, quality, act*	consistency despondency urgency
-end, -and	*to be done*	agenda addenda memorandum
-end, -and	*-ing*	friend fiend errand
endo-	*inside*	endoderm endocranium endocrine
engy-	*near*	engyseismology Engystoma Engyptilla
enigm	*puzzle*	enigma enigmatic enigmatography
enn	see **ann**	

ennea-	*nine* ennead enneagon enneapetalous
ens	*sword* ensiform Ensis ensisternum
-ent	*like, related to, -ing* benevolent consequent nascent
-ent	*one who, that which, -ing* president tangent regent
ent	see **ess**
enter-, entre-	*between* enterprise entertain entrepreneur
enter	*intestine* dysentery enterogastritis enterology
ento-	*within* entozoic entoderm entamoeba
entom	*insect* entomology entomotomy entomophagous
entre-	see **enter-**
eo-	*early, dawn* eolithic eosin Eoanthropus
-eous	*like, having the quality of* igneous aqueous vitreous
ep	*word, tale* epic epos orthoëpy
ep-	see **epi-**
epi-, ep-	*on, outside* epidemic epidermis epitaph
ept	see **apt**
equ	*equal* equation Equator equivocate
equ	*horse* equine equestrian equitation
-er	*more* wiser harder weaker

-er, -yer	*one who, that which*	
	worker lawyer washer	
ere	*sooner, before*	
	ere erstwhile early	
erem	*alone*	
	eremite eremitic hermit	
erg, urg	*work, power*	
	energy ergophobia metallurgy	
-erly	*direction whence*	
	northerly southerly westerly	
-ern	*related to*	
	eastern western leathern	
ero	*to love*	
	erotic erogenous erotomania	
-ero	*one who, that which*	
	torero sombrero vaquero	
err	*to wander*	
	error erratic aberration	
-ery	*place where*	
	bakery brewery bindery	
-ery, -ry	*state, quality, act*	
	slavery drudgery bigotry	
erythr	*red*	
	erythroblast erythrocyte erythroderma	
-escent	*becoming*	
	adolescent obsolescent convalescent	
eschat	*last*	
	eschatology eschatological eschatin	
-ese	*like, related to*	
	Burmese Maltese pekingese	
-esis	*state, quality, act*	
	genesis exegesis poiesis	
eso-	*within*	
	esoteric esoneural esotropia	
eso	see **oiso**	

-esque	*in the manner of*	
	picturesque statuesque Romanesque	
ess, ent	*to be*	
	essential interest entity	
-ess	*feminine*	
	goddess actress mistress	
-est	*most*	
	softest fastest loudest	
esthet, esthes	*feeling*	
	esthetic anesthetic kinesthetic	
-et	see **-ette**	
eth	*character, custom*	
	ethical ethics ethos	
ether	*upper air, to burn*	
	ethereal ethyl ester	
ethm	*sieve, perforated*	
	ethmoid ethmolith ethmosphenoid	
ethn	*race, nation*	
	ethnic ethnology ethnolinguistics	
etio-	*cause*	
	etiology etiogenic etiopathology	
-ette, -et	*little, small*	
	cigarette closet cabinet	
-ety	*state, quality, act*	
	satiety society propriety	
etym	*true*	
	etymology etymologist etymography	
eu-	*good, well*	
	euphony eulogy Eugene	
-eur	*one who*	
	amateur entrepreneur connoisseur	
euro-	*east*	
	Euraquilo Euroclydon Euros	
eurot	*mold*	
	eurodontia eurotophila Eurotia	

eury-	*wide*
	eurycephalic euryplastic eurytopic
euthy-	*straight*
	euthyneura euthyphoria euthoscopic
ev	*age, time*
	medieval longevity primeval
ex-	see **e-**
exo-	*outside*
	exopathic exotic exotoxin
exter-	*outside*
	exterior external extrinsic
extra-	*outward, outside*
	extraordinary extracurricular extralegal
-ez	*descendant of, son of*
	Jimenez Perez Rodriguez

F

fa, fess	*to speak*
	fable nefarious profess
fac, fic, fect, -fy	*to do, to make*
	factory beneficial magnify
fac	*face*
	deface surface facade
falc	*curved, sickle*
	falciform falcate falcular
fall, fals	*to deceive*
	infallible fallacy falsify
fals	see **fall**
far	*flour, grain*
	farina farinaceous farrago
farc	*to stuff*
	farce infarct farctate

fare	*to go* farewell thoroughfare welfare
fasci	*band* fascia fascicle fasciorrhaphy
fatu	*foolish* fatuous fatuity infatuation
fav	*honeycomb* favella faveolate faviform
fe	*cattle, money, property* feudalism fee fellow
febr	*fever* febrile febrifuge febricity
fect	see **fac**
fed	*to feed* fed food foster
fel	*cat* feline feliform felicide
felic	*happy* felicity felicitation infelicitous
femin	*woman* feminine effeminate female
femor	*thigh* femoral femorotibial femorocele
fend	*to strike* fender defend fence
fenestra	*window* fenestral fenestrated defenestration
fer	*to carry* transfer fertile conference
-ferous	*bearing, causing* mortiferous coniferous vociferous
ferr	*iron* ferrous ferroprotein ferriferous
ferv	*to boil, to bubble* fervor fervent effervescent

fess	see **fa**
fest	*feast*
	festive festival festoon
fet	*to stink*
	fetid fetor asafetida
fet	*unborn child*
	fetal fetoplacental effete
fet	see **fot**
fibr	*fiber*
	fibroblast fibrin chondrofibroma
fibul	*pin, buckle*
	fibula fibulocalcaneal Fibularia
fic	see **fac**
fid	*faith*
	fidelity confident infidel
-fid	see **fiss**
fig	*to fashion*
	figure figment effigy
fil	*son*
	filial affiliate FitzGerald
fil	*thread*
	filament file profile
fimbr	*fringe*
	fimbriated fimbriodentate Fimbristylus
fin	*end, limit*
	final infinite definition
firm	*strong*
	confirm infirmary affirm
fiss, -fid	*to split*
	fission fissure bifid
fitz-	*son of*
	FitzGerald Fitzpatrick Fitzsimmons
fix	*to fasten*
	prefix suffix transfix

fla	*to blow* inflate deflate flavor
flabell	*breeze* flabellum flabellifoliate flute
flagell	*whip* flagellant flagellation flail
flagr	*to burn* flagrant conflagration effulgent
flam	*flame* flammable inflammatory flamboyant
flam	see **flem**
flav	*yellow* riboflavin flavid flavescence
flect, flex	*to bend* deflect reflection circumflex
fledge	*feathered, mature* unfledged full-fledged fledgeling
flem, flam	*Flemish* Flemish flamenco flamingo
flex	see **flect**
flict	*to strike* inflict afflict conflict
flor	*flower* floral florist Florida
flot	*to float* float flotilla flotsam
flu, flux	*to flow* fluid superfluous influx
flux	see **flu**
foc	*focus* focal bifocals focimeter
-fold	*-fold, times* tenfold hundredfold manifold
foli	*leaf* foliage exfoliate portfolio

folk	*people*
	folk folklore Volkswagen
foll	*bellows, windbag, bag*
	follicle folly fool
for-	*against, away*
	forbid forsake forswear
for	*door, opening, outdoors*
	perforation forum forest
foramin	*opening*
	foraminal foraminulum Foraminites
-ford	*(river) ford*
	Oxford Stafford Bradford
fore-	*before*
	foresee forewarn forecast
form	*form, shape*
	uniform conformity reformation
formic	*ant*
	formic formicivorous Formica
fornic	*arch*
	fornix fornicate fornicolumn
fort	*strong*
	fortify fortitude comfort
foss	*ditch*
	fossa fossulate fossorial
fot, fet	*foot*
	foot feet fetter
found	see **fund**
found	see **fus**
fract	see **frag**
frag, fract	*to break*
	fragment fraction fracture
franc	*free, French*
	franchise Francis Franco-American
frater	*brother*
	fraternal fraternize confraternity

fre	*to love* free freedom friend
fric	*to rub* friction dentifrice fricative
frig	*cold* frigid frigescent refrigerator
front	*forehead* front confront frontier
fruct	*full enjoyment* fructify fruition fruit
fug	*to flee* fugitive refugee centrifugal
ful	*filthy* foul filth befoul
-ful	*having the quality of* cheerful hopeful remorseful
fulv	*orange* fulvous fulvescent fulvene
fum	*smoke* fume fumigate perfume
fun	*rope* funicular funambulist funiculus
funct	*to perform* function perfunctory defunct
fund, found	*to base, to establish* fundamental foundation profound
fund	see **fus**
furc	*fork* bifurcated furciform furciferous
fus, fund, found	*to pour* transfusion refund foundry
fusc	*dark, tawny* fuscous fuscochlorin fuscoferruginous
-fy	see **fac**

G

gal	*to sing, to scream* gale nightingale yell
galact	*milk* galaxy galactic dysgalactia
gall	*French* Gallic gallium Gallophobe
gam	*marriage* bigamy polygamy monogamous
gangli	*knot* ganglion gangliectomy gangliocyte
gar	*to protect, to supply* garrison garment garnish
gast	*to terrify* ghastly aghast ghost
gastr	*stomach* gastric gastritis gastronomy
ge	*earth* geometry geology apogee
geard	*enclosure, garden* garden yard orchard
gel	*frost* gelid gelatin congeal
gel, gelot	*to laugh* gelotherapy gelometer gelogenic
gelot	see **gel**
gemin	*twin* gemini quadrigeminal gemination
gemm	*bud* gem gemmiform gemmologist
gen	*cause, birth, kind, race* generate homogenized genocide
gen, gon	*knee* genuflection goneitis gonyocele

georg	*farmer* George georgic Georgia
ger	*old* geriatrics gerontology gerontocracy
ger	*spear* Gerald Roger Gerard
ger	see **gest**
geran	*crane (bird)* geranium pedigree crane
germ	*bud* germinal germinate ovigerm
german	*German* Germanic geranium germanite
gest, ger	*to bear, to carry* belligerent congestion gesture
get	*to get* forget beget gotten
gif	*to give* gift given forgive
gigant	*giant* gigantic giganticide gigantomachy
gingiv	*gums* gingivitis gingival gingivolabial
glac	*ice* glacial glacier glaciology
gladi	*sword* gladiolus gladiator gladiatorial
glauc	*gray-green* glaucoma glaucous glauconite
gli	*glue* glioma gliacyte neuroglia
glob	*sphere* globe globule hemoglobin
glochi	*projecting* glochidium glochidial Triglochin

glom *ball of yarn*
glomus   glomerulus   conglomeration

gloss, glot *language, tongue*
glossary   polyglot   epiglottis

glot see **gloss**

gluc see **glyc**

glute *rump, buttocks*
gluteus   gluteal   gluteofemoral

glutin *glue*
gluten   glutinous   agglutination

glyc, gluc *sweet*
glycerine   hypoglycemia   glucose

glyph *to carve*
hieroglyphics   solenoglyph   glyph

gnath *jaw*
prognathous   gnathitis   gnathoplasty

gnom see **gnos**

gnos, gnom *to know*
prognosis   agnostic   gnome

god *God*
goddess   godsend   gossip

gon *angle, corner*
pentagon   trigonometry   orthogonal

gono- *reproductive*
gonophore   gonocyte   gonococcus

gorg *throat*
gorge   disgorge   regurgitate

-gorod see **-grad**

gos *goose*
gosling   gossamer   goosneck

-grad, -gorod *city*
Petrograd   Leningrad   Novgorod

grad, gress *to step*
gradual   graduate   regression

gram	see **graph**
gramin	*grass*
	gramineous graminivorous graminoid
gran	*grain*
	granary granite lipogranuloma
granat	*grainy*
	pomegranate grenade garnet
grand	*great*
	grand aggrandisement grandeur
graph, gram	*to write*
	biography graphite telegram
grat	*free, thankful, pleased*
	gratuity gratitude congratulate
grav	*to dig*
	grave engrave groove
grav	*to weigh, heavy*
	gravity gravitate aggravate
greg	*flock*
	congregation segregate gregarious
gregor	*watchman*
	Gregory Gregorian Grigorevich
gress	see **grad**
grip	*to seize*
	grip gripe grope
gross	*large*
	gross grocer engross
grow	*to grow*
	growth green grass
grund	*bottom*
	ground groundwork groin
guad	*river*
	Guadalupe Guadalajara Guadarama
guan	*dung*
	guano guaniferous guanophore

guerr	*war*
	guerrilla *nom de guerre c'est la guerre*
gust	*taste*
	gusto gustatory disgust
gutt	*drop*
	guttatim gutter gout
guttur	*throat*
	guttural gutturophony gutturonasal
gym	*naked, nude*
	gymnasium gymnospore gymnoblast
gyn	*woman*
	gynecology misogynist gynophobia
gyr	*ring, circle*
	gyration gyroscope gyrospasm

H

hab	*to have*
	habit exhibit ability
haem-	see **hem**
hagi	*holy*
	hagiography hagiarchy hagiolatry
hal	*a salt*
	halide halogen halophile
hal	*whole, healthy, holy*
	hale health halibut
hald	*to hold*
	halt held behold
ham, -heim, home	*home, town*
	Nottingham Mannheim homestead
hang	*to hang*
	hanger hanker hinge
haph	see **hapt**

haplo-   *single*
                                    haploid   haplodont   Haplotaxidae

hapt, haph, aph,   *to touch*
apse   haptephobia   haphalgesia   synapse

hard, -ard   *hard*
                                    hardship   billiards   Leonard

hatch   *to chop*
                                    hatchet   crosshatch   hash

haut   *high*
                                    hauteur   *haute couture*   Terre Haute

hav   *to have*
                                    have   misbehave   behaviorism

hears   *harrow, to harrow*
                                    hearse   rehearse   rehearsal

heart   *heart*
                                    hearty   heartless   dishearten

heath   *wasteland*
                                    heathen   heather   hoyden

hebdomad   *week*
                                    hebdomad   hebdomadal   hebdomadary

hebe   *young*
                                    hebephrenia   hebeanthous   hebetic

hebet   *dull*
                                    hebetude   hebetate   hebetation

hec, hex, ech   *to hold*
                                    hectic   cachexy   epoch

hecto-, hecato-   *hundred*
                                    hectometer   hectograph   hecatomb

hedon   *pleasure*
                                    hedonism   hedonistic   hedonophobia

hedr   *seat, side*
                                    cathedral   polyhedron   sanhedrin

heim   see **-ham**

hel   *to hide*
                                    helmet   hell   hall

heli	*sun*
	heliotrope helium heliocentric
helic	*spiral*
	helicopter helical helix
helminth	*worm*
	helminthiasis platyhelminth Sterelmintha
hem, haem, em	*blood*
	hematology hemorrhage toxemia
hemer	*day*
	ephemeral hemerology hemerobious
hemi-	*half*
	hemisphere hemiplegic hemistich
hen	*one*
	hyphen henogenesis enosis
hepat	*liver*
	hepatic hepatitis gastrohepatic
hept-	*seven*
	heptameter heptatomic heptavalent
her	*to hear*
	hearing hearsay harken
her, hered	*heir*
	inherit heritage heredity
her, hes	*to stick*
	inherent coherence adhesive
herb	*grass*
	herbal herbarium herbivorous
hered	see **her**
herm	*Hermes*
	hermetic hermetically hermaphrodite
herpet	*snake*
	herpes herpetology herpetic
hes	see **her**
hesper	*west, evening*
	Hesperian hesperanopia vespers

hetero-	*other*
	heterogeneous heterodox heterodyne
heur	*to find*
	heuristic heuretic Eureka
hev	*to lift*
	heave heavy upheaval
hexa-	*six*
	hexagon hexahedron hexachlorophene
hiat	*gap*
	hiatus hiatopexia hiation
hibern	*Irish*
	Hibernian Hibernophile Hibernology
hibern	*winter*
	hibernate hibernaculum hibernoma
hidr	*sweat*
	hyperhidrosis hidradenitis hidrocystoma
hier	*sacred*
	hierarchy hieroglyphics hierocracy
hilar	*merry*
	hilarious exhilarate Hilary
hipp	*horse*
	hippopotamus hippodrome Hippocrates
hispan, span	*Spanish*
	Hispanic Hispanophobe spaniel
hist	*tissue*
	histology histogenesis histolysis
hol	*hole*
	hole hollow hold (ship)
hol	*whole*
	holocaust holograph catholic
hol	*whole, healthy*
	holy holiday hollyhock
homo	*man, human being*
	homo sapiens homicide homage

homo-	*same*
	homogeneous homosexual homonym
-hood	*state, quality*
	manhood childhood knighthood
hor	*to bound, to define*
	horizon aphorism aorist
hor	*hour*
	horoscope horology horography
hormon	*to excite*
	hormone hormonology hormonoprivia
horr	*to bristle*
	horror horrible abhorrent
hum	*ground*
	humus exhume humiliate
hum	*liquid*
	humor humidity humidor
hunt	*to pursue, to seize*
	hunter hint hit
hus, hous	*house*
	housewife husband husk
hyal	*glass*
	hyalescence hyalite hyaloid
hydat	*water*
	hydatid hydatism hydatogenesis
hydr	*water*
	hydrant dehydrate hydrogen
hyet	*rain*
	hyetometer hyetology hytography
hygi	*health*
	hygiene hygienic hygeiolatry
hygr	*wet*
	hygrometer hygrology hygrothermal
hyl, yl	*wood, matter, substance*
	hylomorphism hylozoism cacodyl

hymen	*membrane*
	hymen hymenicolar hymenopterous
hyo-	*upsilon-shaped (U)*
	hyoid hyothyroid hyoglossus
hyp-	see **hypo-**
hyper-	*over, above*
	hyperactive hypersensitive hypertension
hyperbor	*north*
	hyperborean hyperboreal Hyperborea
hypn	*sleep*
	hypnotic hypnosis hypnophobia
hypo-, hyp-	*under*
	hypodermic hypofunction hypotenuse
hyps	*high*
	hypsography hypsicephalic hypsodont
hyster	*womb*
	hysteria hysterectomy colpohysteropexy

I

-i	*Latin plural ending*
	alumni cacti radii
-ia	*condition*
	anemia pneumonia tachycardia
-ia	*flower (name)*
	begonia fuchsia dahlia
-iac	see **-ac**
-ian	see **-an**
-iasis	*condition*
	scoleciasis elephantiasis taeniasis
iatr	*healing*
	psychiatrist pediatrician geriatrics
ibi	*there*
	alibi ibid. ibidem

-ible	*able to be* audible visible intangible
-ic	*like, related to* heroic optic rustic
-ical	*like, related to* spherical theatrical juridical
-ice	*act of, time of* service justice novice
ichthy	*fish* ichthyology ichthyosis ichthyoid
icon	*image* iconoclast iconolatry iconostasis
-ics	*science, system* physics ethics linguistics
-id	*like, related to* vivid fluid lucid
id, eid	*to see* idea ideal eidetic
-ida	*group* Arachnida Annelida Tricladida
ident	*same* identity identification identical
ideo-	*idea* ideology ideogram ideogeny
idio-	*personal* idiom idiosyncrasy idiopathic
idol	*image* idolatry idolize idoloclast
-ie	see **-y**
-ier	*one who* cashier courier financier
ig	see **ag**
ign	*fire* ignite ignition igneous

-ik	see **-ek**
il-	see **in-**
-ile	*able to (be)* fertile mobile docile
ile	*ileum, groin* ileostomy ileitis ileocolostomy
-ile	*like, related to* puerile tactile juvenile
ili	*ilium, groin* iliac iliosacral iliofemoral
im-	see **in-**
in	*fiber* inosteatoma initis inogen
in-, im-, il-, ir-	*in, into* inspect incision influx
in-, im-, il-, ir-	*not* incredible intact infidel
incud	*anvil* incus incudiform incudectomy
ind	*Indian* indigo Hindustan Indonesia
indi-	*within* indigenous indigent indigence
indic	*pointer* indication indices index
-ine	*like, related to* masculine bovine saline
infra-	*beneath* infrared infracostal infracortical
insul	*island* insular insulation peninsula
int-	*within* interior internal intestine

integr	*whole*	
	integrity integration integer	
inter-	*between*	
	intercept intermission international	
intra-	see **intro-**	
intro-, intra-	*inside*	
	introduce introvert intramural	
iod, ion	*violet*	
	iodine iodize Ionidium	
-ion, -tion	*state, quality, act, -ing*	
	action diction graduation	
ion	see **iod**	
ir-	see **in-**	
irid	*rainbow, iris (of eye)*	
	iridescent iris keratoiridocyclitis	
ischi	*hip*	
	ischium ischiocele ischialgia	
-ise	see **-ize**	
-ish	*like, related to*	
	foolish boyish boorish	
-ism	*state, quality, act*	
	dogmatism materialism pantheism	
iso-	*equal*	
	isosceles isometric isothermal	
-ist	*one who*	
	dentist militarist misogynist	
it	*to go*	
	exit transit initiate	
ital	*Italian*	
	italics Italic Italo-American	
-ite	*one who*	
	favorite laborite Semite	
-ite	*related to, having the quality of*	
	dendrite polianite porphyrite	

-itious	*having the quality of*
	fictitious excrementitious supposititious
-itis	*inflammation*
	appendicitis arthritis tonsillitis
-ity	*state, quality, act*
	clarity nobility hilarity
-ium	*chemical element*
	helium einsteinium europium
-ive	*one who, that which*
	captive operative missive
-ive	*having the power of*
	explosive productive counteractive
-ize, -ise	*to make, to act*
	fertilizer realize revitalize

J

jac	see **ject**
jan	*doorway*
	janitor January Janus
ject, jac	*to throw*
	reject adjective trajectory
jejun	*fasting, empty*
	jejune jejunum jejunostomy
joan, john	*God's gracious gift*
	Joan Joannine John
joc	*joke*
	jocose juggler jewel
join	see **junct**
journ	*day*
	journal journey adjourn
jov	*Jove (Jupiter)*
	jovial Jovian jovicentric

jud	*Jewish*
	Judaic Judo-Christian Judeophile
jud	*judge*
	judicious judiciary prejudice
jug	see **junct**
junct, jug, join	*to join, to marry, mating*
	conjunction junction conjugal
jur	*to swear*
	juror adjure perjury
juven, jun	*young*
	juvenile rejuvenate junior
juxta	*next to, beside*
	juxtapose juxtaposition joust

K

kary, cary	*nucleus, nut*
	karyosome karyotin caryokinesis
kata-	see **cata-**
kath	see **cath**
ken	see **can**
kerat, cerat	*horn*
	keratolysis keratoma rhinoceros
keraun	see **ceraun**
ket	*acetone*
	ketosis ketonuria ketonemia
kilo-, chilio-	*thousand*
	kilometer kilowatt chiliad
kin	*to beget*
	kinship kindred kind
-kin	*little, small*
	napkin manikin Perkins
kine-, cinema-	*to move*
	kinetic cinema cinematography

klept	*to steal* kleptomaniac kleptophobia biblioklept
know	*to know* knowledge acknowledge known
koni	see **coni**
kre-	see **creat**
kry	see **cry**
krypt	see **crypt**
kym, cym	*wave* kymography kymoscope cymotrichous
kyph	*humpbacked* kyphosis kyphoscoliosis Kyphoclonella

L

la	*people* laity layman Nicholas
lab, lep	*to take, to seize* syllable syllabus epileptic
labi, labr	*lip* labial labiodental labrum
labor	*to work* laborious laboratory Labrador
labr	see **labi**
labyrinth	*maze* labyrinth labyrinthine labyrinthectomy
lac	*milk* lactation lactic lactose
lachrym	see **lacrim**
lack	*loose, to allow* lack slacks lag
lacrim, lachrym	*tear (-drop)* lacrimal lacrimation lachrymose

lacun   *space, hollow*
                             lacuna lacunule Lacunella

laevo-   see **levo-**

laf   *loaf (bread)*
                             loaf lord lady

-lagnia   *lust*
                             osmolagnia coprolagnia pornolagnia

laiss   see **leas**

lal   *to talk, to babble*
                             glossolalia lalopathy Eulalia

lambd   *lambda (λ, Λ), L*
                             lambdoid lambdacism lambdacist

lamell   see **lamin**

lamin, lamell   *leaf, layer*
                             laminated lamellibranch omelet

lan   *wool*
                             lanolin laniferous lanoceric

lanc   *to throw*
                             lance lancet launch

-lani   *heavenly*
                             Leilani Noelani Iwalani

lanthan, lat   *to lie hidden*
                             lanthanum lanthanite latent

lapar   *flank*
                             laparotomy laparocele laparorrhaphy

lapid   *stone*
                             lapidary dilapidated lapidiferous

lapse   *to slip*
                             elapse collapse relapse

larv   *mask, larva*
                             larva larvate larvicide

laryng   *windpipe*
                             laryngitis laryngology laryngectomy

lat	*to carry* translate ventilate legislator
lat	*wide* dilate latitude laticostate
lat	see **lanthan**
later	*side* lateral bilateral laterotorsion
-latry	*worship* idolatory bibliolatry heliolatry
lav, lu	*to wash* lavatory ablution deluge
lax	*loose, to allow* relax laxative languid
leap	*to leap, to run* leap elope gallop
leas, laiss	*loose, to allow* laissez-faire leash lease
lecith	*yolk* lecithin lecithinase lecithal
lect	see **leg**
led	*to lead* leader led load
lef	*to allow, dear* belief love livelong
leg, lig, lect	*to choose, to gather, to read* select eligible illegible
leg	*law* legal legislature legacy
leg	*to lay* lay lie beleaguer
leio-, lio-	*smooth* leiocephalous leiomyosarcoma Liopelmidae
lemm	*skin, rind* lemmocyte neurilemma sarcolemma

| **leni** | *soft, mild* |
| | lenient relentless lenitive |

| **lent** | *lentil* |
| | lens lentiform lenticonus |

| **lent** | *slow* |
| | lentitude lento lentando |

| **leon** | *lion* |
| | leonine Leo leontocephalous |

| **lep, lepid** | *scale* |
| | leper leproma Lepidoptera |

| **lep** | see **lab** |

| **lepid** | see **lep** |

| **lept** | *thin, small* |
| | leptosome leptocephaly leptodermous |

| **lern** | *to teach* |
| | learn learning lore |

| **-less** | *without* |
| | fearless friendless careless |

| **-let** | *little* |
| | booklet cutlet bracelet |

| **leth** | *death* |
| | lethal lethality lethiferous |

| **leth** | *to forget* |
| | lethargy lethargic Lethe |

| **leuc, leuk** | *white* |
| | leucocyte leucoderma leukemia |

| **leuk** | see **leuc** |

| **lev** | *to allow, absence* |
| | leave furlough twelve |

| **lev** | *light (weight), to raise* |
| | alleviate elevator leverage |

| **lev** | *smooth* |
| | levigation levicellular Levipalifer |

levo-, laevo-	*left hand* levoversion levorotatory levophobia
lex	*word, speech* lexicon lexicology lexicographer
-lexia	*to read* bradylexia alexia dyslexia
-ley	*meadow, clearing* Stanley Bradley Beverley
liber	*free* liberate liberal deliver
liber, libr	*weight, balance* deliberate equilibrium lb.
libr	*book* library librarian libel
libr	see **liber**
lic	*to entice, to snare* elicit delicacy delight
lic	*permissible* license illicit licentious
lict	see **linqu**
lid, lis	*to damage* collide elide collision
lien	*spleen* lienal lienorenal lienocele
lif	*life, to live* life lively enliven
lig	*to bind* ligament obligation religion
lig	see **leg**
lign	*wood* ligneous lignescent lignin
liht	*light* light enlighten lightning

lik	*similar* like likeness likewise
limin	*threshold* eliminate preliminary subliminal
limn	*pool* limnology limnobiology limnometer
lin	*flax* linen linoleum linseed
line	*line* lineage delineate patrilineal
-ling	*little* seedling fiingerling fledgeling
lingu	*language, tongue* linguistics bilingual linguopalatal
linqu, lict	*to leave* relinquish delinquent derelict
lio-	see **leio-**
lip, lipo-	*fat* glycolipin lipogenetic lipocardiac
lip	*to leave, to abandon, to lack* eclipse elliptical lipogram
lipo-	see **lip**
liqu	*fluid* liquid liquor liquidate
lis	see **lid**
lit	*bed* litter (bed) litter (offspring) litter (v.)
-lite	*stone* praseolite siderolite physalite
liter	*letter* literal illiterate obliterate
lith	*stone* lithograph monolith paleolithic

littor	*seashore*
	littoral Littorina Littorella
lob	*lobe*
	lobotomy lobulus lobiform
loc	*place*
	local location locomotive
loc	see **loqu**
loft	*air*
	aloft loft lift
log	*word, discourse*
	travelogue monologue eulogy
-logy, -ology	*discourse, study*
	biology geology psychology
long	*long*
	longevity elongate prolong
loqu, loc	*to speak*
	loquacious elocution ventriloquist
los	*to lose*
	loser loss forlorn
lox	*oblique*
	loxodont loxosoma loxodograph
lubr	*slippery*
	lubrication lubricant lubricity
luc	*light*
	lucid translucent lucubrate
lucr	*money, profit*
	lucre lucrative lucrific
luct	*to struggle*
	reluctant ineluctable eluctation
lud, lus	*to play*
	prelude delude collusion
lumb	*loin*
	lumbar lumbago dorsolumbar
lumin	*opening, light*
	lumen luminescence illumination

lun	*moon*
	lunar lunate lunatic
lup	*wolf*
	lupine lupicide lupiform
lus	see **lud**
lute	*yellow*
	luteal luteovirescent luteous
-ly	*having the quality of*
	manly motherly miserly
-ly	*in the manner of*
	childishly wickedly erroneously
lyc	*wolf*
	lycanthropy lycorexia Lycaenidae
lymph	*clear water*
	lymphatic lymphocyte lymphoma
lys, lyt	*to free*
	analysis histolytic electrolyte
lyt	see **lys**

M

-ma	*something done*
	drama stigma diploma
mac, mc	*son of*
	MacDonald McGregor McDaniel
mac	*thin*
	emaciated macilent meager
-machy	*battle*
	sciamachy gigantomachy logomachy
macro-	*big*
	macron macrocosm macroeconomics
macul	*spot, stain*
	immaculate maculocerebral macular

mael	*to grind*	
	maelstrom meal mellow	
mag	*to be able*	
	might may dismay	
magister	*greater, superior*	
	magistrate master mister	
magn-	*great*	
	magnify magnificent magnate	
magnes, magnet	*Magnesia (in Thessaly)*	
	magnesium magnet manganese	
magnet	see **magnes**	
maha-	*great*	
	maharaja mahatma maharani	
major	*larger*	
	majority majordomo mayor	
mak	*to make*	
	maker made match (v.)	
mal	*bad, badly*	
	malformation maladjusted dismal	
malac	*soft*	
	malacoid osteomalacia malacophyllous	
malle	*hammer*	
	mallet malleable malleolus	
mamm	*breast*	
	mammal mammary mammiform	
man	*gas*	
	manometer manograph	
	syphgmomanometer	
man	*man, human being*	
	manslaughter woman manikin	
man	*to stay*	
	permanent mansion remain	
-mancy	*divination*	
	pyromancy necromancy chiromancy	

mand
to entrust, to command
mandate remand mandatory

mandib
lower jaw
mandible mandibuliform
mandibulopharyngeal

mania
craving, insanity
maniac monomania pyromania

manu
hand
manufacture manual manacle

mar
Mars (god)
martial Mars (planet) Mardi Gras

mar
sea
maritime submarine marina

margarit
pearl
margaritiferous Margaret margarine

marit
husband
marital marry mariticide

mark
boundary, sign
mark remarkable demarcation

martyr
witness
martyr martyrdom martyrology

-mas
Mass (ceremony)
Christmas Candlemas Michaelmas

mascul
man
masculine emasculate male

mast
breast
mastitis mastoid mastodon

mater
mother
maternal matrimony matron

math
to learn
mathematics polymath chrestomathy

maur
dark
Mauritania Maurice Moorish

maxill
jaw
maxilla maxillofacial maxillodental

maxim	*largest* maximum maxim maximize
maym	*to mutilate* maim mayhem mangle
maz	*breast* amazon mazopathy mazolysis
mc	see **mac**
mechan	*machine* mechanical mechanic mechanism
med	*to attend to* medicine remedy meditate
med	*middle* medium mediator medieval
medull	*marrow* medulla medullary medullo-arthritis
meg-	see **mega-**
mega-, megal-, **meg-**	*great, million* megaphone megalomaniac megohm
megal-	see *mega-*
mel	*apple* melon marmalade chamomile
mel	*limb* phocomelia anisomelia melagra
mel	*song* melody melodrama melophone
melan	*black* melancholy Melanesia calomel
melior	*better* ameliorate meliorant meliorism
mell	*honey* mellifluous molasses marmalade
membr	*limb, member* member dismember membrane

memor	*to remember*
	memory commemorate memorandum
men	*to lead*
	promenade amenable demeanor
men	*moon, month*
	menopause menorrhea menology
-men	*something done*
	specimen regimen acumen
men	see **mens**
mend	*fault*
	amendment emendation mend
mening	*membrane*
	meningitis meninges meningioma
mens	*to measure*
	dimension immense commensurate
mens	*moon, month*
	menses menstruation mensual
mens	*table*
	mensa commensal mesa
ment	*chin*
	mentolabial mentigerous mentoposterior
ment	*mind*
	mentality demented amentia
-ment	*state, quality, act*
	abasement excitement aggrandizement
-ment	*that which*
	inducement sediment impediment
mer	*to earn*
	merit meritorious meretricious
mer	*part*
	polymerous isomer meroblastic
mer	*thigh*
	merosthenic meralgia merocele
merc	*to trade*
	merchant mercenary market

mercur	*Mercury (god)* mercury mercurial Mercury (planet)
merg, mers	*to dip, to plunge* merger submerge immerse
meridi	*south, noon* meridional meridian a.m.
mers	see **merg**
meso-	*middle* mesoderm mesomorphic Mesopotamia
-mester	*month* semester semestral trimester
met	*to measure, fitting* mete meet (adj.) helpmate
met	*meat, food* meat mate inmate
met	*to meet* meet (v.) meeting moot
met-	see **meta-**
meta-, met-	*beyond, change* metaphor metabolism metamorphosis
meter, metr	*measure* thermometer perimeter asymmetrical
methy	*wine* methyl amethyst methomania
metr	*mother* metropolis metropolitan metropolite
metr	*womb* endometrium metrocele myometrium
metr	see **meter**
mezz	*half* mezzanine mezzo-soprano mezzotint
mi	*less, little* miargyrite Miocene Miohippus

miasm	*pollution*	
	miasma miasmic Miastor	
micro-	*small*	
	microscope microphone microbe	
migra	*to wander*	
	migration emigrate immigrant	
milan	*Milan (Italy)*	
	milanaise Milanese milliner	
milit	*to fight*	
	militant militate militia	
milli-	*thousand*	
	million millimeter millennium	
mim	*to imitate, to copy*	
	mimic mimeograph pantomime	
min	*less, little*	
	diminish minority mince	
min	*to project, to hang over*	
	prominent imminent menace	
minim	*least, smallest*	
	minimum minimize minim	
minister	*to serve*	
	minister administration minstrel	
mir	*to wonder*	
	admire miracle mirror	
mis-	*bad, badly*	
	misinform mispronounce misnomer	
mis-	*to hate*	
	misanthrope misogynist misoneism	
misc	*to mix*	
	miscellaneous miscegenation	
	promiscuous	
miser	*wretched*	
	miser miserable commiserate	
miss	see **mit**	

mit, miss	*to send* transmit missile missionary
mit	*thread* mitochondrion mitosis mitoplasm
mitr	*headband* mitral miter mitella
mix	*to mix* mixotrophic apomixis mixobiosis
mne	*to remember* amnesia mnemonics amnesty
mob	see **mov**
mod	*measure, manner* modest mode accommodate
mol	*to grind (grain)* molar immolate emolument
mol	*heap, burden* demolish molecule molest
moll	*soft* mollify mollusk emollient
molybd	*lead (metal)* molybdenum molybdena molybdic
mon	*moon* Monday month monthly
mon-, ma-	*my* monsignor madam mesdames
mong	*to mix* among mongrel mingle
moni	*to advise, to remind* monitor admonish monument
mono-	*one* monogram monologue monolith
mont	see **mount**
-mony	*state, quality, that which* matrimony acrimony alimony

mor	*custom* mores moral amorality
mor	*stupid* moron sophomore morology
morb	*disease* morbid morbigenous morbose
morph	*form* morphology amorphous metamorphosis
mors, mord	*to bite* morsel remorse mordacious
mort	*death* mortuary mortgage mortal
mot	see **mov**
mount, mont	*hill, mountain* surmount paramount Piedmont
-mouth	*mouth (of river)* Portsmouth Monmouth Plymouth
mov, mot, mob	*to move* move motive automobile
muc	*mucus, moldy, sticky* mucoid mucin mucilage
mucedin	*mildew* mucedinous mucedinaceous mucedine
multi-	*many* multiply multilateral multipurpose
mun	*gift, service* remunerate municipal immune
mund	*clean* mundatory mundificant Mundia
mund	*world* mundane mundanity mundivagant
mur	*wall* mural intramural immure
murn	*to grieve* mourn mourning mournful

mus	*mouse, muscle* musophobia muscle musculature
mus	*one of the nine Muses* music museum mosaic
musc	*a fly* muscicide mosquito musket
mut	*to change* mutation immutable commute
my	*mouse, muscle* myomancy myology myoma
myc	*fungus* mycosis mycelium neomycin
myel	*marrow, spinal cord* myelin myelocyte poliomyelitis
myria-	*countless, ten thousand* myriad myriapod myriameter
myring	*membrane, eardrum* myringa myringitis myringoscope
myrmec	*ant* myrmecology myrmecophagous myrmotherine
mys	*pollution* mysophobia mysophobic mysophilia
myst	*mystery* mystify mystagogue mystical
mytil	*mussel* mytilotoxism Mytilus mytilite
myx	*mucus* myxadenitis myxocyte myxedema

<u>N</u>

n-	*not* never neither none
nam	*name* nameless namesake namely

nan   *dwarf*
                     nanocephalic   nanomelus   nannander

nap   *small sheet*
                     napkin   map   apron

nar   see **nas**

narc   *numbness, stupor*
                     narcotic   narcosynthesis   narcissus

nas, nar   *nose*
                     nasal   nasturtium   nares

nasc   see **nat**

nat, nasc   *to be born*
                     native   nature   nascent

nav   *ship, to sail*
                     navy   navigation   nave

naut   *to sail*
                     nautical   astronaut   nausea

ne-   *not*
                     nefarious   neuter   nescient

nec   see **necr-**

necr-, nec   *death, dead*
                     necrology   necromancy   nectar

nect   *to knot*
                     connect   net   annex

nect   *to swim*
                     nectopod   nectocalyx   Necturus

ned   *need*
                     needy   needless   needful

neg   *to deny*
                     negative   abnegation   negotiate

neigh   *near*
                     neighbor   nigh   next

nemat   *thread*
                     nematode   nemathelminthes   nematocyst

neo-	*new* neon neo-Nazi neologism
nephr-	*kidney* nephrology nephritis nephrolith
nepot	*nephew* nephew nepotism niece
neptun	*Neptune (god)* Neptune (planet) neptunium neptunite
nerv	*nerve* nervous enervate innervate
nes	*island* Polynesia Indonesia Melanesia
-ness	*state, quality* kindness happiness friendliness
neth	*below* nether Netherlands beneath
neur	*nerve* neurology neuralgia neuritis
neutr	*neither* neutral neuter neutroceptor
nickel	*devil, nickel* nickeliferous nickeline nickelous
nictitat	*winking* nictitate nictitation connive
nid	*nest* nidificate nidicolous nidifugous
nigr	*black* Negro negroid denigrate
niht	*night* nightly midnight benighted
-nik	*one who* sputnik beatnik nudnik
nitr	*niter, nitrogen* nitrate nitrous nitrobenzene

niv   *snow*
                     niveous   nivicolous   Nevada

no   *to know*
                     noble   notorious   denote

noc, nox   *to injure*
                     nocent   innocent   innocuous

noc, nox   *night*
                     nocturne   nocturnal   equinox

nod   *knot*
                     node   nodule   nodiflorous

nom   *law, order*
                     astronomy   economy   binomial

nom   see **nomin**

nomin, nom   *name*
                     nomination   misnomer   nominal

non-   *not*
                     nonsense   nonpartisan   nonessential

non   see **novem**

nor-   *north*
                     Norway   Normandy   Norfolk

norm   *a rule*
                     normative   abnormal   enormous

nos   *disease*
                     nosology   nosetiology   nosogeography

nos   *nose*
                     nostril   nosegay   nozzle

noto-   *back (of body)*
                     notochord   notopodium   Notonecta

noto-   *south*
                     Notopithecus   Nototherium   Notogean

nounce   see **nunc**

nov   *new*
                     novelty   renovate   innovation

novem, non	*nine* November novena nonagon
nox	see **noc**
nub, nupt	*to marry* connubial nubile nuptial
nucle	*nut, kernel* nucleus nuclear enucleate
nud	*uncovered* nudiped nudiflorous Nudibranchia
nul	*nothing* nullify annul annulment
numer	*number* numerous numeral enumerate
nunc, nounce	*to announce* enunciate pronounce denounce
nupt	see **nub**
nutri	*to nourish* nutrition nutritive nutriment
nyct	*night* nyctophobia nyctalopia nyctitropic
nymph	*maiden* nymphal nymphlike nympholepsy
nyx	*puncture* pyronyxis scleronyxis Nyxeophilus

O

o'	*grandson of* O'Connor O'Brien O'Malley
ob-, oc-, of-, **op-**	*to, toward, against* object obstacle opposition
obliqu	*oblique* obliquity obliquimeter Obliquaria

obliv	*to forget*	
	oblivion oblivious oblivescence	
oc-	see **ob-**	
occident	*west, falling*	
	occident occidental occidentalize	
occip	*back of head*	
	occipital occiput occipitocervical	
ochlo-	*mob*	
	ochlocracy ochlocrat ochlophobia	
ochr	*yellow, pale*	
	ocher ochroid Ochroma	
-ock	*little*	
	bullock shamrock buttock	
oct-	see **octo-**	
octo-, oct-	*eight*	
	octopus octave October	
ocul	*eye*	
	oculist binoculars monocle	
od, hod	*road*	
	odometer exodus method	
od	*smell*	
	odor malodorous ozone	
od	*song*	
	ode parody rhapsody	
-oda	see **-oid**	
-ode	see **-oid**	
odi	*to hate*	
	odium odious annoy	
odont	*tooth*	
	orthodontist periodontist odontalgia	
odyn	*pain*	
	anodyne arthrodynia neurodynia	
oec	see **eco-**	

oen, en   *wine*
                     oenocyte   oenophilist   enology

of-   see **ob-**

-oid, -oda, -ode *resembling*
                     spheroid   asteroid   nematode

oint   see **unct**

ois, es   *to bear, to carry*
                     Oesophagicola   Stomoisia   esophagus

-ol   see **ole**

ole, -ol   *oil*
                     petroleum   oleomargarine   cholesterol

olfact   *smelling*
                     olfactory   olfaction   olfactometer

oligo-   *few*
                     oligophrenia   oligarchy   oligotrophic

-ology   see **-logy**

olymp   *(Mt.) Olympus*
                     Olympics   Olympiad   Olympian

-oma   *growth, tumor*
                     carcinoma   myoma   sarcoma

ombr   *rain*
                     ombrophilous   ombrometer   ombrifuge

-ome   *group*
                     rhizome   caulome   mestome

omma, ommat   *eye*
                     ommatophore   ommatidium   Loxomma

ommat   see **omma**

omni-   *all*
                     omnipotent   omnivorous   omniscient

omphal   *navel*
                     omphaloskepsis   omphalic
                     Choanomphalus

-on   *Greek ending*
                     criterion   pantheon   phenomenon

onc   *hook*
           onchium   blepharoncus   Oncorhyncus

onc   *mass, tumor*
           oncology   nephroncus   hematoncometry

onoma   see **onym**

ont   *being*
           ontology   ontogeny   sporont

onych   *claw, (finger-)nail*
           onychauxis   leukonychia   anonychia

onym, onoma   *name*
           synonym   anonymous   onomatopoeia

oö-   *egg*
           oölogy   oögenesis   oöcyte

op   *eye, sight*
           optical   optometrist   myopic

op-   see **ob-**

oper   *work*
           operate   cooperation   opera

opercul   *lid*
           operculum   operculate   operculiferous

ophi, ophidi   *snake*
           ophiology   ophidiophobia   Ophelia

ophidi   see **ophi**

ophthalm   *eye*
           ophthalmology   ophthalmic
           ophthalmoscope

opi   *opium*
           opiate   opiomania   opiophagous

opistho-   *back*
           opisthotic   opisthodont   opisthograph

opl   *weapon*
           panoply   anoplocephalic   hoplite

opsi-   *late*
           opsimath   opsiuria   opsigamy

opt	*to choose* option adopt co-opt
optim	*best* optimum optimist optimize
or, os	*mouth* oral orifice osculate
-or	*one who, that which* donor curator tractor
ora	*to speak, to pray* oration oracle inexorable
-orama	*view* panorama diorama cinerama
orb	*circle* orb orbit exorbitant
orch	*to dance* orchestra orchestration Orchestia
orchid	*testicle* orchid cryptorchidism orchidectomy
ordin	*order* coordination subordinate ordination
orex	*appetite* anorexia hyperorexia lycorexia
organ	*instrument* organic organization organon
ori, ort	*to rise, to be born* origin aborigine abortive
orient	*east, rising* orient oriental orientation
-orious	*having the quality of* notorious victorious censorious
-orium	see **-ory**
orn	*to decorate* ornate ornament adornment
ornith	*bird* ornithology ornithoscopy ornithophilous

ort	see **ori**
orth-	*straight, right* orthopedics orthodox orthography
-ory	*like, having the quality of* preparatory regulatory promissory
-ory, orium	*place where* factory lavatory auditorium
os	see **or**
oscill	*to swing* oscillate oscilloscope oscillometer
-ose	*having the quality of* jocose verbose bellicose
-osis, -sis	*condition, act* sclerosis cyanosis analysis
osm	*pushing* osmosis osmotic endosmosis
osm	*smell* anosmia osmesthesia osmium
osphr	*smell* osphretic osphradium osphrencephalon
oss	*bone* ossify ossicle osseous
oste	*bone* osteology osteomyelitis osteopath
osti	*door, opening* ostium ostiary ostiole
ostrac	*shell* ostracize entomostracan Ostracoderm
ot	*ear* otology otitis otoscope
oti	*ease* otiose negotiate negotiable
-otic	*having the quality of, related to* neurotic narcotic psychotic

-ous	*having the quality of* slanderous tortuous amorous
out-	*out* outlaw utter utmost
outr-	see **ultra**
ov	*egg* oval ovary oviparous
over-	*above, too much* overdone overwork overextend
-ovna	*daughter of* Alexandrovna Ivanovna Petrovna
-ow	*having the quality of* mellow yellow callow
own	*to have* owner disown ought
oxy	*sharp, acid* oxygen oxide paroxysm

P

pac	*peace* pacifier pacifist Pacific
pachy-	*thick* pachyderm pachyonchia pachynema
pact	*to agree, to fasten* pact compact impact
pag	see **pec**
pal	*pale* pallor pallid appalling
palai	see **pale**
pale, palai	*ancient* paleolithic paleontology palaiotype
pali	see **palin**

palin, pali	*back, again*
	palindrome palingenesis palinode
pallad	*Pallas (Athena)*
	Pallas (planetoid) palladium palladous
palli	*mantle, cloak*
	palliate pallium palliative
palp	*to pat, feeler*
	palpable palpate palpulus
pan-, panto-	*all*
	panorama pantheon pantomime
pan	*bread*
	pantry company companion
pan	*small cloth*
	pane panel impanel
panto-	see **pan-**
pap, pop	*father*
	papa papal pope
papilion	*butterfly*
	papilionid papilionaceous pavilion
papill	*nipple*
	papilla papilloma papillectomy
par	*to appear*
	apparent apparition appearance
par, part	*to bear*
	parent viviparous parturition
par	*equal*
	parity compare disparage
par	*to prepare*
	pare apparatus separate
par-	see **para-**
para-, par-	*beside, variation*
	paradox parathyroid parenthesis
para	*to prevent*
	parachute parasol parapet

pariet	*wall* parietal parietitis parietofrontal
parl	*word, speech* parley parlor parole
part	*part* participate particolored particle
part	see **par**
parthen	*virgin* parthenon parthenogenesis parthenospore
parv	*small* parvity parvule parvicellular
pass	see **pat**
past	*dough* paste pastry pastel
past	*to feed* pasture pastor repast
pat, pass	*to lie open* patent (adj.) passage patent (v.)
pat, pass	*to suffer* patient passive compassion
patell	*pan, dish* patella patelliform patellofemoral
pater	*father* paternal patriot repatriation
path	*feeling, suffering, disease* apathy sympathetic pathology
path	*path* pathway footpath pathfinder
patul	*spread* patulous patulent Patulaxis
pauci-	*few* paucity pauciloquy paucifoliate
paul	*little* Paul Paulocrinus Pauloscirtes

paul   *pause*
                    paulospore paulocardia Paulomagus

paus   *to cease*
                    pause menopause diapause

pec, pex, pag   *to fasten*
                    pectin hepatopexy thoracopagus

pectin   *comb*
                    pectinate pectiniform pectineal

pector   *chest*
                    pectoral expectorate pectoriloquy

pecu   *money, cattle, property*
                    pecuniary impecunious peculation

ped   *child*
                    pediatrician pedagogue orthopedist

ped   *foot*
                    pedal pedestrian impede

ped   *ground*
                    pedology pedograph pedogeography

pedicul   *louse*
                    pediculosis pediculicide pediculophobia

pel, puls   *to push*
                    propel expulsion repulsive

pel   *skin*
                    pelt pellagra surplice

pel-   see **per-**

pelag   *sea*
                    archipelago pelagic bathypelagic

pelecy   *hatchet*
                    pelecoid Pelecypoda Pelecystoma

pelv   *basin*
                    pelvis pelvic pelviform

pen   *almost*
                    peninsula penultimate peneplain

pen   *punishment*
                    penalty penance repent

pen	*tail, penis* pencil Penicillium penicillin
pend, pens	*to hang, to weigh, to pay* pendulum pensive compensation
-penia	*to need, to lack* thrombopenia erythrocytopenia eosinopenia
penn	see **pinn**
pens	see **pend**
penta-	*five* pentagon pentameter pentathlon
peps	see **pept**
pept, peps	*to digest* peptic dyspepsia eupeptic
per-, pel-	*through, intensive* permit perspire pellucid
per	*to try out* experience expert peril
perei	*to transport* pereiopod pereion Pereionotus
peri-	*around* periscope perimeter perigee
persic	*Persian* Persic Persicaria peach
pest	*plague* pest pestilence pestiferous
petal	*leaf, thin plate* petal petalite petalodont
petit	*to seek* petition competitor appetite
petit	*small, little* petite petticoat petty
petr	*rock* petroleum petrify Peter

pex	see **pec**
pha	see **phe**
phac, phak	*lentil, lens* phacolith phacosclerosis phakitis
phag	*to eat* sarcophagus esophagus anthropophagous
phalang	*in ranks* phalanx phalange brachyphalangia
phall	*penis* phallus phallic phalloid
phan, phen	*to show, to appear* diaphanous phantom phenomenon
phaner	*visible* phanerocryst phanerogam phaneroscopy
pharmac	*drug* pharmacy pharmacist pharmaceutical
pharyng	*throat* pharyngeal pharyngitis pharyngectomy
phas	see **phe**
phe, phas	*to say, to speak* prophesy euphemism aphasia
phen	see **phan**
pher	see **phor**
phil	*to love* philanthropist philosopher Philadelphia
phleb	*vein* phlebitis phlebology phlebotomy
phlegm	*flame* phlegm phlegmatic adenophlegmon
phlog	*flame* phlogiston antiphlogistic phlogocytosis
phob	*to fear* claustrophobia acrophobia hydrophobia

phoc   *seal (animal)*
                      phocine   phocomelia   Phocodontia

phoenic   *red*
                      phoenix   phoenicite   Phoenicopterus

phon   *sound*
                      phonograph   telephone   cacophony

phor, pher   *to carry*
                      phosphorus   semaphore   Christopher

phos   see **phot**

phot, phos   *light*
                      photograph   photosynthesis   phosphorus

phragm, phrax   *fence, enclosure*
                      diaphragm   phragmoplast   emphraxis

phras   *speech*
                      phrase   phraseology   periphrasis

phren   *brain*
                      phrenology   schizophrenic   frantic

phthis   *to waste away*
                      phthisic   ophthalmophthisis   phthisiology

phthong   *voice, sound*
                      diphthong   phthongometer   aphthongia

phyl   *tribe, race, phylum*
                      phylum   phylogeny   Phylarchus

phylac   *guard*
                      prophylactic   anaphylaxis   phylactery

phyll   *leaf*
                      chlorophyll   phyllophagous   phyllopod

phym   *growth*
                      phymatosis   arthrophyma   phymatodes

phys   *bellows, bladder*
                      physocele   emphysema   physalite

physi   *nature, natural*
                      physics   physiology   physique

phyt   *plant*
                      phytology   neophyte   phytogenesis

pi   *holy, tender*
                    pious   pity   *pia mater*

picr   *bitter*
                    picrodendron   picrite   chloropicrin

pict   *to paint*
                    picture   depict   pigment

pil   *ball*
                    pill   pellet   piles

pil   *hair*
                    depilatory   caterpillar   pillage

pin   *pine cone*
                    pineal   pinoid   pinetum

pinn, pinnat,   *feather*
penn   pinniform   pinnatiped   pennoplume

pinnat   see **pinn**

pisc   *fish*
                    piscatorial   piscine   Pisces

pithec   *ape*
                    cercopithecus   Pithecanthropus
                    Australopithecus

pituit   *phlegm*
                    pituitary   pituitous   pituicyte

plac   *flat*
                    placodont   placoderm   placoplast

plac   *to please*
                    placid   implacable   complacent

placent   *flat cake*
                    placenta   extraplacental   placentoid

plagi   *oblique*
                    plagioclase   plagiocephalic   plagiograph

plain   *to lament*
                    complain   plaintive   plaintiff

plan   *flat, soft (sound)*
                    plain   plane   piano

plan	*to wander* planet aplanobacter planogamete
plant	*sole of the foot* planta plantar plantigrade
plas	*to form* plastic plaster protoplasm
platin	*silver, platinum* platinum platiniridium platinate
platy-	*flat, broad* platypus platyhelminth platyrrhine
plaud	*to strike, to applaud* plaudit plausible explode
-ple	*-fold, times* triple quadruple multiple
ple, plei	*more* pleonasm pleodont pleiomery
pleb	*people* plebiscite plebeian plebicolar
plect	*twisted* Plectanella Plectaster Plectognathi
pleg	*stroke, paralysis* hemiplegia paraplegia plegometer
plei	see **ple**
plen, plet, -ply	*full* plenitude complete supply
pless	see **plex**
plet	see **plen**
pleth	*full* plethora plethysmograph Plethodon
pleur	*side, rib* pleurisy pleurodont pleuroperitoneum
plex, plic, -ply	*to fold* complex explicit multiply

plex, pless	*to strike* apoplexy pleximeter plessigraph
plic	see **plex**
plor	*to cry* implore deplore explore
plum	*feather* plume plumage plumiped
plumb	*lead (metal), plumb-line* plumber plumb plummet
plur	see **plus**
plus, plur	*more* plus surplus plurality
plut	*Pluto (god)* Pluto (planet) plutonium plutonic
plut	*wealth* plutocrat plutocracy plutology
pluvi	*rain* pluviometer pluvial plover
-ply	see **plen**
-ply	see **plex**
pne	see **pneumon**
pneumon, **pneum, pne**	*to breathe, lung* pneumonia pneumatic traumatopnea
pock	*sack* pocket pockmark pouch
pod, pus	*foot* tripod chiropodist octopus
poe	see **poie**
pogon	*beard* pogonology pogoniasis Calopogon
poie, poe	*to make, to produce* sarcopoietic hematopoiesis poet
pol	*axis of a sphere* pole polar peripolar

pol	*to polish* polish polite politesse
pol	*Polish* polonaise polonium polka
poli, polit	*city, state* politics polity police
poli	*gray* poliomyelitis polianite Polianthes
-polis	*city* metropolis cosmopolitan Annapolis
polit	see **poli**
poll	*head* poll polls tadpole
poly-	*many* polygon polytheism polygamy
poly	*to sell* monopoly monopolistic oligopoly
pom	*fruit, apple* pomiferous pommel pomegranate
pon, pos	*to place, to put* postpone deposit proposition
ponder	*weight* ponder ponderous preponderant
pont	*bridge* pontoon pontocerebellar pontiff
pop	see **pap**
popul	*people* population populace popular
por	*callus* porocele porokeratosis porosis
por	*opening, passage* pore porous blastopore
porn	*prostitute* pornography pornocracy pornolagnia

porphyr	*violet*
	porphyry porphyrin porphyrogen
port	*to carry*
	report transportation deportee
port	*harbor, gate*
	port portal opportune
pos	see **pon**
pos	see **pot**
poss	see **pot**
post-	*after*
	postpone post-mortem posthumous
poster-	*behind, after*
	posterior posterity preposterous
pot, poss	*to be able*
	potent potentate possible
pot, pos	*to drink*
	potion symposium poison
potam	*river*
	hippopotamus potamology Mesopotamia
potass	*potash, potassium*
	potassium potassic potassamide
poul	*chicken*
	poultry pullet polecat
-poulos	*son of*
	Constantinopoulos Giannopoulos Georgiopoulos
pract, prax	*to do*
	practical apraxia pragmatic
prae-	see **pre-**
pras	*green*
	praseodymium praseolite prasine
prav	*crooked*
	depraved depravity depravation
prax	see **pract**

pre-, prae-	*before* preview predict praesidium
prec	*to pray* imprecate deprecate precarious
preci	*price* precious appreciate depreciate
pred	*booty* predatory depredation prey
prehend, **prehens, pris**	*to take, to seize* comprehend apprehension prison
prehens	see **prehend**
presby	*old* presbyophrenia presbyopia Presbyterian
press, print	*to press* impress depression reprint
preter-	*beyond* preternatural preterite pretermission
prim, prin	*first* primary primitive principal
prin	see **prim**
print	see **press**
pris	see **prehend**
priv	*single, separate* private privilege deprive
pro-	*for, before, forward* program provision progress
prob	*to test, good* probation approbation prove
proct	*anus* proctology proctodynia periproct
prol	*offspring* prolific proliferate proletariat
prometh	*Prometheus (Greek hero), provident* Promethean promethium Promethichthys

propr	*one's own*
	proprietor property appropriate
pros-	*front, forward*
	prosopyle prosenchyma prosthermotaxis
prosop	*face*
	diprosopus prosopalgia Prosopothrips
proto-	*first*
	proton prototype protozoa
prox	*near*
	proximity approximate proximal
pseud	*false*
	pseudonym pseudoscience pseudopod
psor	*itch*
	psoriasis psorosperm Psoraphora
psych	*mind*
	psychology psychiatry psychosomatic
psychr	*cold*
	psychrometer psychrograph psychrophilic
pter	*feather, wing*
	pterodactyl helicopter pterosaur
pterid	*fern*
	pteridophyte pteridography pteridoid
pto	*to fall*
	ptomaine symptom nephroptosis
ptyal	*spittle*
	ptyalism ptyalin ptyalocele
pub	*mature, pubic*
	puberty pubescent pubofemoral
pud	*to be ashamed, to be modest*
	impudent pudent pudenda
pugn	*to fight*
	pugnacious repugnant pygmy
pulchr	*beauty*
	pulchritude pulchritudinous pulchrify

pulm, pulmon	*lung* pulmonary pulmolith pulmotor
pulmon	see **pulm**
puls	see **pel**
pulver	*dust* pulverize pulvereous powder
pulvin	*cushion* pulvinus pulvinate pulvillus
pun	*to punish* punish punitive impunity
punct	see **pung**
pung, punct	*to prick* pungent puncture compunction
pupa	*doll, child* puppet pupil pupa
pur	*clean* pure purify purification
pur, pus	*foul matter* purulent suppurate pustule
purg	*to clean* purge purgative unexpurgated
purpur	*purple* purpura purpurogenous purpurescent
pus	see **pod**
pus	see **pur**
put	*to prune, to correct* amputate impute compute
putr	*rotten* putrid putrescent putrefaction
py	*pus* pyorrhea pyosis pyemia
pycn	*thick* pycnic pycnometer Pycnogonida

pyel	*	*trough, basin*
		pyelometry pyelogram nephropyelitis
pyg		*buttocks*
		callipygian steatopygous Macropygia
pyl		*gate*
		pylorus micropyle pylangium
pyr		*fire*
		pyromaniac pyrotechnics pyrography
pyr		*pear*
		pyriform Pyrola Pyroplasma
pyren		*fruit-stone*
		pyrenoid pyrenolysis pyrenocarp
pyret		*fever*
		pyretogenesis antipyretic pyretetiology

Q

quadr-, quart	*four*
	quadruplets quadrangle quarter
qual	*what kind*
	quality qualify qualifications
quant	*how much*
	quantity quantitative quantum
quart	see **quadr-**
quer	*to complain*
	querulous quarrel querimonious
quest, quir, quis	*to ask, to seek*
	question inquire inquisitive
quies, quiet	*to rest*
	acquiesce quiet acquit
quiet	see **quies**
quinqu-, quint-	*five*
	quintuplets quintet quintessence
quint-	see **quinqu-**

quir	see **quest**
quot	*how many*
	quota quotient quotennial

R

rab	*rabies*
	rabid rabigenic rabiform
rach, rrhach	*spine*
	rachitic rachiodont hematorrhachis
rad	*ray*
	radiation radium radius
rad	see **ras**
radic	*root*
	radical eradicate radish
ram	*branch*
	ramification ramiform ramigerous
ran	*frog*
	ranunculus ranine Ranidae
rap	*to snatch, to seize*
	rapid rapacity rape
raph, raphid, -rrhaph	*to sew, suture*
	raphides rhapsody gastrorrhaphy
raphid	see **raph**
ras, rad	*to scrape*
	erase abrasive abrade
rat	*to reckon, to reason*
	rational ratify ratio
re-	*back, again*
	report retract recurrent
re	*thing*
	republic real reify
rec	*to stretch*
	reach overreach rack

reck	*to heed*
	reckon reckoning reckless
rect	*to rule, straight, right*
	rector direct rectify
red	*to interpret*
	read reader riddle
red	*red*
	redden ruddy rusty
reg	*to rule, straight, right*
	regime region regulate
rem	*oar*
	trireme quinquereme remiform
ren	*kidney*
	renal adrenalin renoparietal
rept	*to creep*
	reptile reptant surreptitious
ret	*net*
	retothelium retina reticulate
retro-	*backwards*
	retrogression retrospect retroactive
rev	see **rob**
rhabd	*rod*
	rhabdocoele rhabdolith rhabdomancy
rhen	*Rhine (River)*
	Rhenish rhenium Rhineland
rhin	*nose*
	rhinoceros rhinitis rhinoscope
rhiz	*root*
	rhizopod hydrorhiza rhizophagous
rhod	*red*
	rhododendron rhodium Rhode Island
rhomb	*to spin*
	rhombus rhomboid rhombiform

rhynch   *snout*
     rhynchophorous   rhyncholite
     Trypanorhyncha

rhyt, rut   *wrinkle*
     rhytidome   rhytidectomy   rutidosis

rhythm   *measured flow*
     rhythmic   rhythmometer   rhyme

rid, ris   *to laugh*
     ridiculous   deride   derision

rid   *to ride*
     rider   road   raider

rip, riv   *(river-)bank*
     riparian   rival   derivation

ripe   *ripe*
     ripen   reap   reaper

ris   *to rise*
     arise   raise   rouse

ris   see **rid**

-rix, -trix   *feminine*
     aviatrix   mediatrix   executrix

ro   *fame*
     Robert   Roger   Roland

rob   *oak, strong*
     robust   corroboration   corroborative

rob, rev   *to rob, booty*
     robbery   robe   bereave

rode, ros   *to gnaw*
     rodent   corrode   erosion

rog   *to ask*
     interrogate   prerogative   arrogant

roll, rol   *to roll*
     role   controller   roulette

roman   *Roman*
     romance   romaine   Rumania

ros	*rose, red* rosaceous rosy rosary
ros	see **rode**
rost	*gridiron* roster roast roaster
rostr	*beak, prow* rostrum rostrate rostellum
rot	*wheel, to turn* rotate rotary rotund
rrhach	see **rach**
-rrhage, -rrhex	*to burst, to flow* hemorrhage menorrhagia metrorrhexis
-rrhaph	see **raph**
-rrhea	*to flow* pyorrhea diarrhea logorrhea
-rrhex	see **-rrhage**
rub	*red* ruby rubella rubric
rud	*crude* rude erudition rudimentary
ruf	*red* rufous ruficaudate Rufus
rug	*wrinkle* rugate ruga Rugaceae
rugh	*shaggy* rough rug ragged
run	*to run* outrun runway runaround
rupt	*to break* interrupt abrupt rupture
rur	see **rus**
rus, rur	*country*

russ	*Russia* Russo-Japanese Russophile Russophobe
rut	see **rhyt**
ruthen	*Russia* ruthenium ruthenic Ruthenia
rutil	*red, orange* rutilant rutile rutin
-ry	see **-ery**

S

-s	*son of* Roberts Williams Jones
sac	*bag* sac sack satchel
sacchar	*sugar* saccharine saccharic sacchariferous
sacr	*sacred* sacrifice sacrilege sacrosanct
sal, sil, sult	*to leap* salient resilient insult
sal	*salt* saline salinometer salary
salic	*willow* salicylic salicetum salicin
salping	*tube, trumpet* salpingitis salpingectomy salpingopexy
salut	*health* salutary salute salutation
salv	*safe* salvation salvage savior
san	*healthy* sane sanitary sanitarium

san, sant	*saint, holy*
	San Francisco Santa Clara Santa Claus
sanct	*holy*
	sanctify sanctuary sanctimonious
sanguin	*blood*
	sanguine sanguinary consanguinity
sant	see **san**
sap	*soap*
	saponaceous saponify soap
sap	*taste, judgment*
	homo sapiens savor insipid
sapr	*putrid*
	sapremia saprophyte saprozoic
sarc	*flesh*
	sarcophagus sarcoma sarcastic
sardin	*Sardinia*
	sardine sardonic Sardinian
sat	*enough*
	satisfy saturate insatiable
saturn	*Saturn (god)*
	saturnine Saturday sapphire
saur	*lizard*
	dinosaur ichthyosaurus sauropod
sax	*rock*
	saxifrage saxigenous Saxicola
sax	*(made by Adolphe) Sax*
	saxophone saxhorn saxtuba
say	*to declare*
	saying sage saw (proverb)
scala	*ladder*
	scalar escalator escalation
scand	*Scandinavia*
	Scandia Scandian scandium
scandal	*stumbling-block*
	scandalous scandalize slander

| **scaph** | *hollow, boat* |
| | scaphoid   scaphocephaly   Scaphella |

| **scapul** | *shoulder blade* |
| | scapular   scapulet   scapulo-clavicular |

| **scat, skat** | *dung* |
| | scatological   scatophilia   skatole |

| **scel** | *dry* |
| | Sceletomerus   Sceliphron   skeleton |

| **scel** | *leg* |
| | isosceles   scelotyrbe   Scelidosaurus |

| **scen** | *(stage-) set* |
| | proscenium   scenario   scene |

| **scend, scens, scent** | *to climb* |
| | descend   condescension   ascent |

| **scens** | see **scend** |

| **scent** | see **scend** |

| **schemat** | *form, figure* |
| | schematic   schematograph   scheme |

| **schis** | see **schiz** |

| **schiz, schis** | *to split* |
| | schizophrenia   schism   schist |

| **schol** | *leisure* |
| | scholar   scholastic   school |

| **sci** | *to know* |
| | science   omniscient   conscious |

| **sci, ski** | *shadow* |
| | sciamachy   skiameter   squirrel |

| **sciat** | *hip* |
| | sciatic   sciatica   sciatical |

| **scintill** | *spark* |
| | scintilla   scintillating   scintillometer |

| **scirrh** | *hard* |
| | scirrhoid   scirrhogastria   mastoscirrhus |

scler   *hard*
  sclerosis   scleroid   scleroderma

scolec   *worm*
  scolex   scoleciasis   scolecoidectomy

scoli   *crooked*
  scoliosis   scoliometer   scolion

scop   *to look*
  microscope   telescope   cystoscope

scor   *notch*
  score (n.)   score (v.)   score (twenty)

scot   *darkness*
  scotopic   scototherapy   scotophobia

scrap   *to scrape*
  scraper   scrap   scramble

scrib, script   *to write*
  prescribe   inscription   manuscript

script   see **scrib**

sculp   *to carve*
  sculptor   sculpture   scalpel

scut   *shield*
  scutiform   scutate   squire

scyph   *cup*
  scyphus   scyphozoan   scyphistoma

se-   *apart*
  secure   secluded   segregation

seb   *fat*
  sebaceous   sebum   seborrhea

sebast   *honored*
  Sebastopol   Sebastian   Sebastichthys

sec   see **sect**

sec   see **sequ**

sec   see **sicc**

sect, sec   *to cut*
  dissect   intersection   secant

| **sed, sid, sess** | *to sit* |
| | sedentary   preside   session |

| **see** | *to see* |
| | unforeseen   overseer   sight |

| **seism** | *to shake* |
| | seismology   seismograph   tachyseism |

| **selen** | *moon* |
| | selenium   selenology   selenophobia |

| **sell** | *to sell* |
| | seller   sold   sale |

| **sem** | *sign, meaning* |
| | semaphore   semantics   semeiography |

| **semi-** | *half* |
| | semiannual   semifinal   semiconscious |

| **semin** | *seed* |
| | seminal   dissemination   seminar |

| **sen** | *old* |
| | senior   senile   senator |

| **-sen** | see **-son** |

| **sens, sent** | *to feel* |
| | sensation   sensitive   sentiment |

| **sent** | see **sens** |

| **seps, sept** | *putrid* |
| | asepsis   antiseptic   septicemia |

| **sept-** | *seven* |
| | septennial   September   septet |

| **sept** | *wall* |
| | septum   septobranch   septonasal |

| **sept** | see **seps** |

| **septentrion** | *north* |
| | septentrion   septentrional   septentrionaline |

| **sequ, sec** | *to follow* |
| | consequence   sequence   persecute |

ser	*series*
	serial insert dissertation
ser	*watery fluid*
	serum serology seroculture
seric	*silk*
	sericeous sericiculture sericite
serr	see **serrat**
serrat, serr	*a saw*
	serrated serrate Serricornia
serv	*to serv*
	service servile subservient
sesqui	*one-and-one-half*
	sesquicentennial sesquipedalian
	sesquiquadrate
sess	see **sed**
set	*bristle*
	seta setobranch setaceous
set	see **sit**
sever	*serious*
	severe persevere asseverate
-sex	*Saxon*
	Sussex Wessex Middlesex
sex-	*six*
	sextet sextant siesta
shad	*shade*
	shady shadow shed (n.)
shake	*to shake*
	shaky shock Shakespeare
shape	*form*
	shapely misshapen leadership
shear, shor	*to cut, to divide*
	shears plowshare shore
shin	*to shine*
	shiny shone shimmer

-ship	*state, quality* hardship friendship partnership
shire	*county* sheriff Shropshire Cheshire
shor	see **shear**
shot	*to shoot, to throw* shoot (v., n.) shut sheet
show	*to look at* show showy sheen
shrub	*bush* shrub shrubbery scrub (adj.)
shuf	*to push* shove shovel shuffle
sial	*saliva* polysialia sialolith sialogram
sib	*relative* sibling sibmate (n., v.) gossip
sicc, sec	*dry* desiccate siccative demi-sec
sid	see **sed**
side	*side* besides sideways inside
sider	*iron* siderolite siderosis siderocyte
sider	*star* sidereal sideromancy siderostat
sigm	*like a sigma (S), related to sigma* sigmoid sigmodont sigmatic
sign	*sign* signal designate resignation
sil	see **sal**
silic	*flint, silicon* silicone silica siliceous

silv, sylv	*forest* silvan Pennsylvania savage
sim	*snub-nosed* simian Simobison Simosaur
simil	*like* similar simile assimilate
sin	*Chinese* sinology Sinanthropus Sino-European
sine	*without* sinecure *sine qua non sine die*
sing	*to sing* singer sang songstress
sinistr	*left hand* sinister sinistral sinistrorse
sinu	see **sinus**
sinus, sinu	*hollow, curve* sinus sinuous sinupalliate
siphon	*tube* siphon siphonophore siphonostele
-sis	see **-osis**
sist	*to stand, to set* resistant consistency persist
sit, siti	*food, grain* parasite sitology sitiomania
sit, set	*to sit, to set* sitting settee settlement
siti	see **sit**
skat	see **scat**
skep	*to look at, to examine* skeptic omphaloskepsis skepticism
ski	see **sci**
sla	*to strike, to slay* slayer slaughter sly

slav	*Slavic* Slavo-Germanic Slavophile slave
slid	*to slide* slid slither sled
slip	*to glide* slip slippers slippery
slow	*slow* slowly sloth slothful
smith	*worker* blacksmith locksmith wordsmith
snak	*to creep* snake sneak snail
soci	*companion* society association dissociate
sod	*soda, sodium* sodic sodalite sodiohydric
sol	*alone* solo sole solitary
sol	*flat ground* sole (of foot) sole (fish) soil (ground)
sol	*sun* solar solarium solstice
solen	*pipe, channel* solenoid solenoglyph typhlosole
solid	*solid* consolidate solder soldier
solu	see **solv**
solv, solu	*to free* solvent resolve solution
som, somat	*body* chromosome psychosomatic somatogenic
somat	see **som**
-some	*having the quality of* worrisome burdensome lonesome

somn	*sleep*
	somnolent insomnia somnambulist
-son, -sen	*son of*
	Anderson Richardson Hansen
son	*sound*
	resonance unison dissonant
soph	*wise*
	sophomore philosopher sophisticated
sor	*painful*
	sore soreness sorry
soror	*sister*
	sorority sororicide sororiation
sort	*lot, chance*
	consort assortment sorcery
soter	*safety, salvation*
	soteriology soterial creosote
soth	*true*
	soothsayer forsooth soothe
sour	*sour*
	sourdough sauerkraut sorrel (plant)
span	see **hispan**
spasm	*convulsion*
	spasm spasmodic spastic
spec, spic	*to look*
	spectator inspector perspicacity
spek	*to speak*
	speaker speech spoke
spel	*cave*
	speleology spelunker speleothem
spell	*to recite*
	spell (magic) spell (v.) gospel
sper	*to hope*
	desperate despair prosper

sperm, spermat	*seed*
	spermatozoon spermatogenesis
	spermatophyte
spermat	see **sperm**
spers	*to strew*
	aspersion disperse sparse
sphen	*wedge*
	sphenoid disphenoid sphenogram
spher	*ball*
	hemisphere spheroid spherical
sphincter	*band*
	sphincter sphincteral sphincteroplasty
sphing, sphinx	*to bind*
	sphinx sphingometer sphingiform
sphygm	*pulse*
	asphyxiate sphygmomanometer
	sphygmograph
spic	see **spec**
spin	*to spin*
	spindle spinster spider
spin	*thorn, spine*
	spiny cerebrospinal porcupine
spir	*breath, life*
	spirit perspire inspiration
spir	*a coil*
	spiral aspirin spirochete
splanchn	*viscera*
	splanchnic splanchnolith splanchnocele
splen	*spleen*
	splenic splenomegaly hypersplenia
splend	*to shine*
	splendid splendor resplendent
spond, spons	*to pledge*
	respond sponsor spouse

spondyl *vertebra*
spondylotherapy   spondylopathy
Paleospondylus

spong *sponge*
spongiculture   spongophore
neurospongium

spons see **spond**

spor *to sow, seed*
spore   sporadic   sporophyte

spuri *false*
spurious   spuriae   Spuriostyloptera

squam *scale*
squamous   squama   squamoparietal

sta, stit *to stand, to set*
stable   status   constitution

stagn *pool*
stagnant   stagnate   tank

stal see **stol**

stalagm, stalact *dripping*
stalagmite   stalactite   stalactiform

stall *place*
pedestal   forestall   installment

-stan *country*
Pakistan   Afghanistan   Hindustan

stan see **ston**

stann *tin*
stannum   stannous   stannic

staped *stirrup-bone*
stapediform   stapedectomy   stapes

staphyl *bunch of grapes*
staphylococcus   staphylodermatitis
staphylectomy

star *stiff, to die*
stare   starve   stern (adj.)

stasis, stat	*standing* prostate hemostat thermostat
stead	*place* steadfast homestead Hampstead
stear	see **steat**
steat, stear	*fat* steatopygous stearic stearate
steg	*roof, covering* stegosaurus branchiostegal Stegocephalia
-stein	*stone* Edelstein Goldstein Silverstein
stell	*star* stellar constellation stellate
sten	*narrow* stenographer stenotopic stenosis
-ster	*one who, woman who* teamster prankster Baxter
ster	*to steer* steerage astern starboard
ster	see **stereo-**
sterc	*dung* stercoral stercoraceous stercorite
stereo-, ster	*three-dimensional, solid* stereophony stereotype cholesterol
stern	*chest, breast* sternum sternotomy sternocostal
steth	*chest, breast* stethoscope stethometer stethophone
sthen	*strong* calisthenics asthenic neurasthenic
sti	*to go up* stirrup stile stair
stib	*mark, antimony* stibium stibnite stibine

stich	*line* hemistich distich acrostic
stig, sting, stinct	*to prick, to mark* instigate stigma distinction
stik	*to pierce* stick stitch sting
stil	*a drop* distil distillery instil
stinct	see **stig**
sting	see **stig**
stip	*to press together* constipate stipulate stevedor
stip	*stem* stipe stipule stipuliferous
stir	*to disturb* stir bestir stormy
stirp	*stem, stock* stirps stirpiculture extirpate
stit	see **sta**
-stle	see **stol**
stol, stal, -stle	*to send* systole peristalsis apostle
stom	*mouth, opening* stomach Chrysostom colostomy
ston, stan	*stone* stony Stanley Stanford
stor	*to set up* store restoration restaurant
strat	*army* strategy stratagem stratocracy
strat	*to spread* prostrate stratification street
strec	*to stretch, to extend* stretcher straight straggler

streph	see **stroph**
strept	see **stroph**
stria	*channel* stria striated striation
strict	see **string**
string, strict	*to tie* stringent district constriction
strobil	*twisted, pine cone* stroboscope strobila strobiliferous
stront	*Strontian (in Scotland), strontium* strontia strontian strontianite
stroph, streph, strept	*to turn* catastrophe strephosymbolia streptococcus
struct	*to build* structure obstruct instruction
stult	*stupid* stultify stultiloquence stolid
stup	*struck dumb* stupor stupid stupendous
sty	*enclosure* pigsty steward Stuart
styl	*column, pen* styloglossus peristyle stylus
su-	*south* Sussex Surrey Suffolk
suad, suas	*to advise, to persuade* persuade dissuade suasion
suas	see **suad**
suav	*sweet, agreeable* suave assuage sweet
sub-, suc-, suf-, sug-, sup-, sur-	*under* submarine supposition surreptitious
suc-	see **sub-**

sud	*sweat* sudatory sudatorium sudarium
suf-	see **sub-**
sug-	see **sub-**
sui	*self* suicide suicidal *sui generis*
sulc	*furrow* sulcus sulciform sulcate
sulf, sulph	*sulfur* sulfate sulphuric Solferino
sulph	see **sulf**
sult	see **sal**
sum, sumpt	*to take* presume resume consumption
summ	*highest point, sum* summarize summit consummation
sumpt	see **sum**
sup-	see **sub-**
super-, supra-, sur-	*over, above* superior suprarenal survive
supra-	see **super-**
sur-	see **sub-**
sur-	see **super-**
swer	*to swear* answer forswear sworn
swet	*sweet* sweeten sweetheart sweetmeat
sy-	see **syn-**
syl-	see **syn-**
sylv	see **silv**
sym-	see **syn-**

syn-, syl-, sym-, **sys-, sy-**	*with, together* synchronization sympathy systole
syring	*pipe* syringe syringium syringomyelia
sys-	see **syn-**

_T_

ta	see **ton**
tab	*wasting* tabes tabescent taboparalysis
tabl	*plank* table tablet tabulate
tac, tic	*silent* tacit taciturn reticent
tach	*fast* tachycardia tachometer tachistoscope
tact	see **tang**
tact	see **tax**
taen	*ribbon, tapeworm* taenia taeniasis taeniola
tail	*to cut* detail retail tailor
tain	see **ten**
tal	*ankle* talipes talotibial talon
tal	see **dal**
tal	see **tell**
tang, tact	*to touch* tangible intact contact
tann	*tanbark* tan tannic tawny

tantal   *(King) Tantalus*
               tantalize   tantalum   tantalus

tapet   *carpet*
               tapetum   tapetal   tapesium

taph   *tomb*
               epitaph   cenotaph   taphephobia

tard   *late, slow*
               tardy   retard   retardation

tars   *instep, (edge of) eyelid*
               tarsus   metatarsal   tarsoplasty

taur   *bull*
               tauromachy   Minotaur   toreador

tauto-   *same*
               tautology   tautonym   tautomerism

tax, tact   *arrangement*
               syntax   taxidermist   tactics

tech   *to show, to guide*
               teach   taught   token

techn   *art, skill*
               technology   technique   pyrotechnic

tect   *builder*
               architect   architectonic   tectology

tect   see **teg**

-teen   *and ten*
               thirteen   fifteen   nineteen

teg, tect   *to cover*
               protege   protect   detective

tele, teli, telo *end, completion*
               teleology   teliospore   telophase

tele-   *from afar*
               television   telephone   telemetric

teli   see **tele**

tell, tal   *to count, to relate*
               teller   tale   talk

tellur	*earth, tellurium* telluric tellurous telluriferous
telo	see **tele**
temper	*proper mixture* temperate temperance temper (n., v.)
tempor	*time* temporary contemporary temporize
tempt	*to try* tempt attempt tentative
ten, tin, tain	*to hold* tenacious abstinence retain
ten, tenon	*stretched tight* tenodynia tenonitis tenontagra
ten	*ten* tenth fifteenth tithe
tend, tens, tent	*to stretch* tendency extensive attention
tens	see **tend**
tent	see **tend**
tenu	*thin* tenuous attenuate extenuating
ter	*three* ternary tertiary tertian
terat	*monster* teratism teratology teratoma
terg	*back (of body)* tergiversation tergum tergal
term	see **termin**
termin, term	*end, limit* terminal determine exterminate
terr	*earth* territory Mediterranean terrier
terr	*to frighten* terror terrify deterrent

tes	*to pluck* tease tousle tussle
test	*testicle* testitis testibrachium testicond
test	*witness* testify testament protest
tetan	see **ton**
tetra-	*four* tetragon tetrameter tetrasyllabic
text	*to weave* text texture textile
-th	*state, quality, that which* health truth birth
thalam	*(inner) chamber* thalamus hypothalamus thalamencephalon
thalass, thalatt	*sea* thalassiophyte thalassiarch thalattology
thalatt	see **thalass**
thall	*twig, thallium* thalloid thallophyte thalliferous
than	see **thanat**
thanat, than	*death* thanatopsis thanatophobia euthanasia
thaum	*miracle* thaumaturge thaumatology thaumotrope
the, theo	*God* theology atheist Theodore
the	*to look at* theater theory theorem
thec	*case* theca apothecary endothecium
thel	*nipple* thelitis thelerethism epithelium

theo	see **the**
ther	*beast* theriatrics theriomorphic therolatry
therap	*treatment* therapy therapeutic hydrotherapy
therm	*heat* thermometer thermostat diathermy
thes, thet	*to place, to put* thesis antithesis synthetic
thet	see **thes**
thi	*sulfur* thiamine thiazole thiogenic
thigm	*to touch* thigmotaxis thigmotropism thigmocyte
think	*to seem, to appear* think thought thanks
thirst	*thirst* thirst thirsty athirst
thor	*Thor (god)* thorium thorite Thursday
thorac	*chest* thorax thoracic thoracoplasty
-thorpe	see **-dorf**
thrall	*slave* thrall thralldom enthralled
thrill	*to pierce* thrill thrilling nostril
thrix	see **trich**
thromb	*clot* thrombus thrombosis thrombokinase
thur	*incense* thurifer thurible thurification
thym	*spirit* thymogenic thymotactic dysthymia

thym	*thymus (gland)*
	thymic thymin thymocyte
thyr	*shield, thyroid*
	thyroid thyreosis thyrosis
tibi	*shinbone, flute*
	tibia tibiotarsus Tibicen
tic	see **tac**
tim	*to fear*
	timid intimidate timorous
tim	*honor*
	timocracy Timothy Timarcha
tin	see **ten**
tinct	see **ting**
ting, tinct	*to dye*
	tinge tincture taint
-tion	see **-ion**
titan	*Titan*
	titanic titanium Titanosaurus
tme	see **tom**
toc, tok	*childbirth, child*
	dystocia epitokous mogitocia
tok	see **toc**
tol	*to raise, to support*
	extol toll tolerate
tom, tme	*to cut*
	atom anatomy tmesis
ton, ta, tetan	*stretching, tone*
	monotone ectasis tetanus
ton	*to thunder*
	detonate astonish stun
-ton	*town*
	Washington Boston Carrolton
tons	*to shear, to clip, to cut*
	tonsure tonsorial tonsor

top　　　　　*place*
　　　　　　　　topology topography isotope

tor　　　　　*to twist*
　　　　　　　　contortion distort torture

torp　　　　*numb*
　　　　　　　　torpor torpid torpedo

torr　　　　*to burn*
　　　　　　　　torrid torrent thirst

tot　　　　　*entirely*
　　　　　　　　total totalitarian totipotential

tourn　　　*to go around*
　　　　　　　　tournament return attorney

tox　　　　　*poison*
　　　　　　　　antitoxin toxemia intoxicate

tra-　　　　see **trans-**

trache　　　*windpipe*
　　　　　　　　trachea tracheoscopy tracheotomy

trachel　　　*neck*
　　　　　　　　trachelopexy trachelology trachellate

trachy　　　*rough*
　　　　　　　　trachyglossate trachyte trachea

tract　　　　*to drag, to draw*
　　　　　　　　tractor extraction tractable

trag　　　　*goat*
　　　　　　　　tragedy tragic tragicomedy

trans-, tra-　　*across*
　　　　　　　　transport trans-Atlantic travesty

traumat　　　*wound, blow*
　　　　　　　　trauma traumatic traumatophobia

treg　　　　*trillion*
　　　　　　　　tregadyne tregerg tregohm

trem, trom　　*to shake*
　　　　　　　　tremble tremendous tromometer

tremat　　　*hole*
　　　　　　　　trematode trematodiasis Trematonotus

trench, trunc   *to cut*
       trench   trenchant   truncated

trepan, trypan   *to bore*
       trepan (n., v.)   trepanation   trypanosome

tri-   *three*
       tripod   trident   trigonometry

trib   *to bestow, to share*
       contribution   tributary   retribution

trib   see **trip**

tric   *petty obstacle*
       extricate   intricate   intrigue

trich, thrix   *hair*
       trichina   trichinosis   trichomycosis

trip, trib   *to rub*
       entripsis   tripsacum   nototribe

trit   *to rub*
       trite   contrite   detriment

-trix   see **-rix**

troch   *wheel, pulley*
       trochaic   trochophore   truck

trochanter   *runner*
       trochanter   trochantin   trochanteroplasty

trogl   *hole*
       troglodyte   troglobiont   troglotrema

trom   see **trem**

-tron   *suffix from "electron"*
       cyclotron   betatron   bevatron

trop   *to turn*
       tropical   heliotrope   trophy

troph   *to nourish*
       trophic   atrophy   hypertrophy

tru   *faithful*
       truth   trust   betrothed

trud, trus	*to thrust* intrude extrude protrusion
trunc	see **trench**
trus	see **trud**
trypan	see **trepan**
tu	*to guard, to look at* tutor tuition intuition
tub	*pipe* tube tuba tubule
tuber	*bump, swelling* tuberous tuberculosis protuberance
-tude	*state, quality, act* servitude latitude magnitude
tum	*to swell* tumor tumescent tumultuous
tunic	*mantle* tunicate tunicin Tunicata
turb	*to agitate* turbulence disturb perturbation
turbin	*to spin* turbine turbinal turbinectomy
turk	*Turkey* turkey Turkish turquoise
turr	*tower* turret turrilite tower
tus	*to pound* contusion obtuse pierce
twi-	*two* twin twilight twine
-ty	*state, quality, that which* liberty beauty property
-ty	*times ten* thirty fifty seventy
tympan	*drum* tympany tympanum tympanectomy

typ *model, impression*
typical   prototype   archetype

typh *fog, stupor*
typhus   typhoid   adenotyphus

typhl *blind*
typhlosole   typhlostomy   typhlectasis

tyr *cheese*
tyrosine   tyroid   tyrogenous

tyrann *tyrant*
tyrannical   tyrannicide   tyrannophobe

U

ubiqu *everywhere*
ubiquity   ubiquitous   ubiquist

ul *gums*
ulothrophia   uloncus   ulocarcinoma

ul *scar*
ulosis   uloid   ulotomy

-ula see **-ule**

-ule, -ula *small*
spherule   capsule   gastrula

-ulent *having the quality of*
corpulent   virulent   truculent

uln *elbow*
ulna   ulnar   ulnoradial

-ulous *having the quality of*
ridiculous   fabulous   bibulous

ultim *last*
ultimate   ultimatum   penultimate

ultra-, outr- *beyond*
ultraviolet   ultramodern   outrage

-um *Latin ending*
modicum   pendulum   interregnum

| **umbilic** | *navel* |
| | umbilicus   umbilical   umbilectomy |

| **umbr** | *shade* |
| | umbrella   umbrage   adumbration |

| **un-** | *not* |
| | unhappy   uncertain   unmitigated |

| **unct, oint** | *to oil* |
| | unction   ointment   anoint |

| **und** | *wave* |
| | inundate   abundant   redundant |

| **-und** | see **-cund** |

| **under-** | *beneath* |
| | undergo   undertake   understand |

| **ungul** | *hoof, claw* |
| | ungulate   ungulifolia   unguligrade |

| **uni-** | *one* |
| | uniform   unison   unilateral |

| **-uous** | *having the quality of* |
| | impetuous   tortuous   sumptuous |

| **ur** | *tail* |
| | anurous   urochord   squirrel |

| **ur, uret** | *urine* |
| | urology   urogenital   urethra |

| **uran** | *sky, heavens* |
| | Uranus   uranium   uranography |

| **urb** | *city* |
| | urban   urbane   suburban |

| **-ure** | *state, quality, act* |
| | departure   rupture   primogeniture |

| **-ure** | *that which* |
| | creature   furniture   debenture |

| **uret** | see **ur** |

| **urg** | see **erg** |

| **urin** | *urine* |
| | urinalysis   urinology   uriniferous |

urs   *bear (animal)*
                        ursine   *Ursa Major*   ursiform

-us   *Latin ending*
                        focus   gladiolus   impetus

us, ut   *to use*
                        abuse   utensil   utility

ut   *out*
                        utter (adj.)   utter (v.)   utmost

ut   see **us**

uter   *uterus, womb*
                        uterine   uterocele   uterolith

utop   *no-place*
                        Utopia   utopian   utopographer

utricul   *small bag*
                        utricle   utricular   Utricularia

uvul   *little grape*
                        uvula   uvulitis   uvulectomy

uxor   *wife*
                        uxorial   uxorious   uxoricide

V

vac   *empty*
                        vacant   evacuate   vacation

vacc   *cow*
                        vaccine   vaccinate   vaccination

vad, vas   *to go*
                        invade   evade   pervasive

vag   *to wander*
                        vagrant   vagabond   extravagant

vagin   *sheath*
                        vagina   vaginal   vanilla

val   *to be strong*
                        valid   value   equivalent

val	*valley*
	vale valley avalanche
valv	*folding door*
	valve bivalve valvular
van	*empty*
	vanish evanescent vanity
vanad	*Vanadis (goddess), vanadium*
	vanadic vanadiferous vanadite
vap	*steam*
	vapor evaporate vapid
var	*diverse*
	various variety variegate
varic	*(dilated) vein*
	varicose varicotomy varicoid
variol	*pox*
	variola variolate variolite
vas	*vessel*
	vascular vasectomy vasoconstrictor
vas	see **vad**
vect	see **veh**
veg	*to enliven*
	vegetation vegetate vegetable
veh, vect	*to carry*
	vehicle vehement convection
vel	*veil, covering*
	velum velar revelation
veloc	*fast*
	velocity velocipede velocimeter
ven	*to come*
	convention revenue intervene
ven	*vein*
	venesection venous venation
vend	*to sell*
	vend vendor venal

venen	*poison*
	veneniferous venom veneno-salivary
vener	*sexual*
	venereal venery venerologist
vent	*wind*
	ventilator ventilation ventometer
ventr	*stomach*
	ventral ventriloquist ventrotomy
ver	*true*
	verify verdict veracious
verb	*word*
	verbal adverb verbiage
verg	*to lean*
	verge converge divergent
verm	*worm*
	vermin vermiform vermicelli
verruc	*wart*
	verruca verrucous verruciform
vers	see **vert**
vert, vers	*to turn*
	revert advertise versatile
vertebr	*joint, vertebra*
	vertebra vertebrectomy invertebrate
vesic	*bladder, blister*
	vesicle vesicant vesicular
vest	*to dress*
	vest vestment investment
vestig	*footprint*
	vestige vestigial investigate
vet	*old*
	veteran inveterate veterinary
via	*way, road*
	via viaduct trivial
vic	*substitute*
	vicarious vicar vice-president

-vich	*son of*
	Ivanovich Petrovich Grigorevich
vicin	*neighbor*
	vicinity vicinal vicinage
vict	see **vinc**
vid, vis	*to see*
	provide television invisible
vig	*lively*
	vigilant vigil vigorous
vil	*cheap*
	vile vilify vilification
vill	*country dwelling*
	village villa villain
vill	*velvet, shaggy*
	villus villiform velvet
-ville	*city, town*
	Abbeville Joinville Placerville
vin	*wine*
	vintage vinegar viniculture
vinc, vict	*to conquer*
	convince invincible victorious
vinc, vict	*conqueror*
	Vincent Victor Victoria
violac	*violet*
	violaceous violescent Violaceae
vir	*man*
	virile triumvirate virtue
vir	*poison, virus*
	virus virulent virology
virid	*green*
	viridescent viridity viridigenous
vis	see **vid**
visc	*sticky*
	viscous viscosity viscid

viscer	*belly, internal organs* visceral visceromotor viscerotome
vit	*grapevine* viticulture viticetum vitiferous
vita	*life* vital vitamins revitalize
vitell	*yolk* vitellus vitelline vitellaria
vitr	*glass* vitreous vitrify vitriol
viv	*to live* revive vivid vivisection
voc, voke	*voice, to call* vocal vociferous revoke
vol	*to will* volunteer volition benevolent
volu	see **volv**
volv, volu	*to roll* revolve evolution volume
vomer	*plowshare* vomer vomerine vomeronasal
vor	*to eat* voracious carnivore omnivorous
vot	*to vow* vote votive devotion
vulcan	*Vulcan (god)* vulcanize volcano volcanology
vulg	*common* vulgar divulge Vulgate
vuln	*wound* vulnerable invulnerable vulture
vulp	*fox* vulpine vulpecide Vulpes
vuls	*to tug* convulse convulsion revulsion

W

wak	*to be awake* awaken watch wait
wal	*foreign, Celtic* walnut Wales Walloon
war	*aware* wary unaware beware
ward	*to protect* warden wardrobe reward
-ward	*toward* upward windward backward
warf	*to turn* wharf whirl whorl
warn	*to protect* warning warrant warranty
weiss	*white* edelweiss Weisshorn bismuth
wer	*to wear* wearer wore worn
whisk	*to flick* whisk whiskers whisk-broom
-wich, -wick	*town* Norwich Sandwich Warwick
-wick	see **-wich**
wif	*female* wife wifely woman
wis	see **wit**
-wise	*in the manner of* clockwise likewise lengthwise
wit, wis	*to know* witty witness wisdom
with-	*against* withstand withdraw withhold

worth	*value*	
	worthy worship stalwart	
wring	*to twist*	
	wring wrong wrench	
writh	*to twist*	
	writhe wrath wreath	
wroht	*to work*	
	wrought cartwright playwright	

X

xanth	*yellow*	
	xanthous xanthophyll xanthoderma	
xen	*foreign, strange*	
	xenophobia xenolith xenon	
xer	*dry*	
	xerophilous xerophagous xerography	
xiph	*sword*	
	xiphoid xiphophyllous xiphocostal	
xyl	*wood*	
	xylophone xyloma xylography	

Y

-y	*having the quality of*	
	gloomy dirty hasty	
-y, -ie	*small*	
	doggy kitty Maggie	
-y	*something done*	
	injury augury colloquy	
-y	*state, quality, act*	
	melancholy history astronomy	

-yer	see **-er**
yl	see **hyl**
ytterb	*Ytterby (in Sweden)* ytterbium yttrium terbium

Z

zeal	*fervor* zealot zealous jealous
zephyr	*westwind* zephyr zephyrean Zephyranthes
zeug	see **zyg**
zinc	*zinc* zincite zinciferous zincography
zircon	*zircon* zirconium zirconate zirconic
zo	*animal* zoology protozoon spermatozoon
-zoic	*animal, life* cytozoic Cenozoic Mesozoic
zon	*belt* zone zonal zonoplacental
zyg, zeug	*yoke, paired* zygote heterozygous zygodactyl
zym	*ferment* enzyme zymology zymurgy

SECTION 2

English-to-Roots

A

to abandon	*lip*
abdomen	*abdomin*
able to (be)	*-able*
able to be	*-ible*
able to (be)	*-ile*
to be able	*mag*
to be able	*pot, poss*
above	*hyper-*
above	*over-*
above	*super-, supra-, sur-*
absence	*lev*
abundance	*copi*
acetone	*ket*
acid	*acid*
acid	*oxy*
acorn	*balan*
across	*trans-, tra-*
act	*-acy, -cy*
act	*-age*
act	*-ance*

act	*-ancy*
act	*-asia, -asis*
act	*-asm*
to act	*-ate*
act	*-ence*
act	*-ency*
act	*-ery, -ry*
act	*-esis*
act	*-ety*
act of	*-ice*
act	*-ion, -tion*
act	*-ism*
act	*-ity*
to act	*-ize, -ise*
act	*-ment*
act	*-osis, -sis*
act	*-tude*
act	*-ure*
act	*-y*
to adjust	*apt, ept*
to advise	*moni*
to advise	*suad, suas*
from afar	*tele-*
after	*post-*
after	*poster-*
again	*ana-*
again	*palin, pali*
again	*re-*
against	*ad-*
against	*anti-, ant-*
against	*contra-, counter-*

against	*for-*
against	*ob-, oc-, of-, op-*
against	*with-*
age	*ev*
to agitate	*turb*
to agree	*pact*
agreeable	*suav*
air	*aer*
air	*aur*
air	*loft*
all	*omni-*
all	*pan-, panto-*
to allow	*lack*
to allow	*lax*
to allow	*leas, laiss*
to allow	*lef*
to allow	*lev*
almond	*amygdal*
almost	*pen*
alone	*erem*
alone	*mono-*
alone	*sol*
amber	*electr*
America	*americ*
amnion	*amni*
amoeba	*amoeb*
ancient	*pale, palai*
angel	*angel*
angle	*angul, angl*
angle	*gon*
animal	*zo*

animal	*-zoic*
ankle	*tal*
ankle-bone	*astragal*
to announce	*nunc, nounce*
to anoint	*unct, oint*
anointed	*christ*
ant	*formic*
ant	*myrmec*
antimony	*stib*
anus	*an*
anus	*proct*
anvil	*incud*
apart	*se-*
ape	*pithec*
Aphrodite	*aphrodis*
to appear	*par*
to appear	*phan, phen*
to appear	*think*
appetite	*orex*
to applaud	*plaud*
apple	*mel*
apple	*pom*
arc	*arc*
arch	*fornic*
area	*chor*
arm	*brac*
arm	*brachi*
arms	*arm*
arms	*opl*
army	*strat*
around	*ambi-, amphi-*

around	*circum-*
around	*peri-*
to go around	*tourn*
arrangement	*tax, tact*
arsenic	*arsen*
art	*art*
art	*techn*
artery	*arter*
ash	*ciner*
to be ashamed	*pud*
to ask	*bid, bead*
to ask	*quest, quir, quis*
to ask	*rog*
ass	*asin*
to assess	*cens*
at	*a-*
Athena	*athen*
Atlas	*atlant*
atrium	*atri*
to attend to	*med*
awake	*vig*
to be awake	*wak*
aware	*war*
away	*ab-*
away	*apo-, ap-*
away	*cata-, cath-, cat-*
away	*de-*
away	*dis-, di-, dif-*
away	*e-, ex-*
away	*ec-*
away	*for-*

away	*se-*
axis	*ax, axon*
axis	*pol*

B

to babble	*lal*
Bacchus	*bacch*
bacillus	*bacill*
back	*ana-*
back	*back*
back (of body)	*dors*
back (of body)	*noto-*
back	*opistho-*
back	*palin, pali*
back	*re-*
back (of body)	*terg*
backwards	*retro-*
spherical bacterium	*cocc*
bad	*cac*
bad	*dys-*
bad	*mal*
bad	*mis-*
badly	*dys-*
badly	*mal*
badly	*mis-*
bag	*asc*
bag	*bel*
bag	*bulg*
bag	*burs*

bag	*foll*
bag	*sac*
small bag	*utricul*
to bake	*bak*
balance	*liber, libr*
ball	*ball*
ball of yarn	*glom*
ball	*pil*
ball	*spher*
band	*fasci*
band	*sphincter*
to banish	*ban*
(river-) bank	*rip, riv*
bare	*gym*
bare	*nud*
bark	*cortic*
to base	*fund, found*
basin	*pelv*
basin	*pyel*
battle	*-machy*
to be	*ess, ent*
beak	*rostr*
bear (animal)	*arct*
to bear	*ber*
to bear	*gest, ger*
to bear	*lat*
to bear	*ois, es*
to bear	*par, part*
to bear	*phor, pher*
to bear	*port*
bear (animal)	*urs*

to bear	*veh, vect*
beard	*pogon*
bearing	*-ferous*
beast	*ther*
beautiful	*bell*
beautiful	*calli*
beauty	*cosmet*
beauty	*pulchr*
becoming (proper)	*dec*
becoming	*-escent*
bed	*lit*
bedbug	*cimic*
bee	*api*
before	*ante-*
before	*anter-*
before	*ere*
before	*fore-*
before	*pre-, prae-*
before	*pro-*
to beget	*kin*
behind	*aft*
behind	*poster-*
being	*ont*
to believe	*cred*
bell	*calyc*
bell	*campan*
bellows	*foll*
bellows	*phys*
belly	*coeli*
belly	*viscer*
below	*hypo-, hyp-*

below	*infra-*
below	*neth*
below	*sub-, suc-, suf-, sug-, sup-, sur-*
below	*under-*
belt	*cinct*
belt	*zon*
bench	*bank*
to bend	*bow*
bend	*croc*
to bend	*flect, flex*
beneath	*hypo-, hyp-*
beneath	*infra-*
beneath	*neth*
beneath	*sub-, suc-, suf-, sug-, sup-, sur-*
beneath	*under-*
Bengal (India)	*bengal*
berry	*bacc*
berry	*cocc*
beside	*juxta-*
beside	*para-, par-*
best	*optim*
to bestow	*trib*
better	*melior*
between	*dia-, di-*
between	*enter-, entre-*
between	*inter-*
beyond	*meta-, met-*
beyond	*preter-*
beyond	*ultra-, outr-*
big	*macro-*
big	*magn-*

big	*maha-*
big	*mega-, megal-, meg-*
bigger	*major*
biggest	*maxim*
bile	*bil*
bile	*chol*
to bind	*bind*
to bind	*cinct*
to bind	*lig*
to bind	*sphing, sphinx*
to bind	*string, strict*
bird	*avi*
bird	*ornith*
birth	*gen*
birth	*toc, tok*
to bite	*mors, mord*
bitter	*alum*
bitter	*amar*
bitter	*picr*
black	*atr*
black	*melan*
black	*nigr*
bladder	*cyst*
bladder	*phys*
bladder	*vesic*
blame	*culp*
blind	*caec, cec*
blind	*typhl*
blister	*vesic*
blood	*bled, blod*
blood	*hem, haem, em*

blood	*sanguin*
blood vessel	*angi*
to blow	*blaw*
to blow	*fla*
a blow	*traumat*
blue	*caes, ces*
blue	*cerule*
blue	*cyan*
board	*barr*
board	*bord*
board	*tabl*
boat	*cymb*
boat	*scaph*
body	*corp*
body	*som, somat*
to boil	*ferv*
bond	*clam*
bond	*copul*
bond	*des, dem*
bone	*oss*
bone	*oste*
book	*bibli*
book	*libr*
booty	*pred*
booty	*rob, rev*
to bore (through)	*trepan, trypan*
to be born	*nat, nasc*
to be born	*ori, ort*
both	*ambi-, amphi-*
bottom	*basi*
bottom	*byss, byth*

bottom	*edaph*
bottom	*grund*
to bound	*hor*
boundary	*mark*
bow	*arc*
bowl	*amni*
bowl	*cymb*
box	*caps*
brain	*cerebr*
brain	*encephal*
brain	*phren*
branch	*ram*
bread	*pan*
to break	*brek*
to break	*clas*
to break	*frag, fract*
to break	*rupt*
breast	*brest*
breast	*mamm*
breast	*mast*
breast	*maz*
breast	*stern*
breast	*steth*
breath	*anim*
breath	*atm*
breath	*spir*
to breathe	*pneumon, pneum, pne*
breathless	*asthm*
breeze	*aur*
breeze	*flabell*
bridge	*-bridge, -bruck*

bridge	*pont*
bright	*agla*
bright	*bert*
bristle	*chaet, chet*
to bristle	*horr*
bristle	*set*
broad	*brad*
broad	*platy-*
bronze	*aene*
bronze	*chalc*
brother	*adelph*
brother	*frater*
brown	*aeth*
brown	*brun*
bubble	*bull*
to bubble	*ferv*
buckle	*fibul*
bud	*blast*
bud	*gemm*
bud	*germ*
to build	*struct*
builder	*tect*
bull	*taur*
bump	*tuber*
burden	*mol*
to burn	*arid*
to burn	*burn, bran*
to burn	*caust, caut*
to burn	*ether*
to burn	*flagr*
to burn	*torr*

burnt	*aeth*
to burn up	*combur*
to burst	*-rrhage, -rrhex*
bush	*shrub*
butter	*butyr*
butterfly	*papilion*
buttocks	*glute*
buttocks	*pyg*
to buy	*cheap*
to buy	*empt*

C

(Julius) Caesar	*caesar*
to call	*voc, voke*
callus	*por*
camp	*-caster, -cester*
canal	*canal*
cancer	*cancer, chancr*
cancer	*carcin*
cape	*cap*
carbuncle	*anthrac*
card	*cart*
care	*cur*
carpet	*tapet*
to carry	*ber*
to carry	*fer*
to carry	*gest, ger*
to carry	*lat*
to carry	*ois, es*
to carry	*phor, pher*

to carry	*port*
to carry	*veh, vect*
cartilage	*chondr*
to carve	*glyph*
to carve	*sculp*
case	*thec*
cat	*ailur, aelur*
cat	*cat*
cat	*fel*
head of cattle	*capit*
cattle	*fe*
cattle	*pecu*
cause	*etio-*
cause	*gen*
causing	*-ferous*
cave	*spel*
cavern	*antr*
to cease	*paus*
cell	*cell*
cell	*cyt*
Celtic	*wal*
center	*centr*
cerebrum	*cerebr*
Ceres	*cere*
chain	*caten*
chalk	*cret*
chamber	*camer*
(inner) chamber	*thalam*
chance	*sort*
change	*amoeb*
change	*meta-, met-*

to change	*mut*
channel	*solen*
channel	*stria*
character	*eth*
charcoal	*carbo*
charge	*crimin*
cheap	*vil*
cheek	*bucc*
cheese	*case*
cheese	*tyr*
chemical element	*-ium*
chest	*pector*
chest	*stern*
chest	*steth*
chest	*thorac*
chicken	*poul*
(unborn) child	*fet*
child	*ped*
child	*pup*
child	*toc, tok*
childbirth	*toc, tok*
children	*prol*
chin	*ment*
China	*sin*
chi-shaped (X)	*chias*
to choose	*leg, lig, lect*
to choose	*opt*
to chop	*hatch*
Christ	*christ*
church	*eccles*
cilium	*blephar*

circle	*cycl*
circle	*gyr*
circle	*orb*
citizen	*civ*
citrus	*citr*
city	*-abad*
city	*-grad, gorod*
city	*poli, polit*
city	*-polis*
city	*urb*
city	*-ville*
clavicle	*clavic*
clavicle	*cleid, cleis*
claw	*chel*
claw	*onych*
claw	*ungul*
clean	*clean*
clean	*mund*
clean	*pur*
to clean	*purg*
clear	*clar*
clearing	*-ley*
to climb	*scend, scens, scent*
to clip	*tons*
cloak	*palli*
to close	*clud, clus, claus, close*
clot	*thromb*
cloth	*cloth*
small cloth	*pan*
clothes	*vest*
clothing	*dysi*

club	*clav*
club	*coryn*
coal	*anthrac*
coal	*carbo*
coast	*cost*
cobalt	*cobalt*
cock	*alector, alectry*
coil	*spir*
cold	*col, chil*
cold	*cry, kry*
cold	*crym*
cold	*frig*
cold	*psychr*
color	*chrom, chro*
color	*color*
column	*styl*
comb	*cten*
comb	*pectin*
to come	*come*
to come	*ven*
to command	*mand*
common	*cen, coen*
common	*vulg*
companion	*comit*
companion	*soci*
to complain	*quer*
completion	*tele, teli, telo*
condition	*-ia*
condition	*-iasis*
condition	*-osis, -sis*
cone	*con*

to conquer	*vinc, vict*
conqueror	*vinc, vict*
container	*caps*
contest	*athl*
convulsion	*spasm*
to cook	*coct*
copper	*aene*
copper	*chalc*
copper	*cupr*
to copy	*mim*
coral	*corall*
corner	*gon*
correct	*orth-*
to correct	*put*
correct	*rect*
to count	*tell, tal*
countless	*myria-*
country	*rus, rur*
country	*-stan*
country dwelling	*vill*
county	*shire*
course	*drom*
to cover	*cover*
to cover	*teg, tect*
covered	*calypt*
(hard) covering	*crust*
covering	*steg*
covering	*vel*
cow	*bou, bov*
cow	*vacc*
crab	*cancer, chancr*

crab	carcin
to crack	crak
to crack	crepit
to crackle	crepit
craft	art
craft	techn
crane (bird)	geran
craving	mania
to creep	rept
to creep	snak
crime	crimin
to croak	crek
crooked	ankyl, ancyl
crooked	kyph
crooked	prav
crooked	scoli
cross	cruc
crossbar	cancel
crown	coron
crude	rud
to cry	plor
crystal	cryst
cuckoo	coccyg
cup	calyc
cup	cotyl
cup	cyath
cup	scyph
curl	cirr, cirrh
curv	sinus, sinu
curved	campt
curved	campyl

curved	*curv*
curved	*falc*
cushion	*pulvin*
custom	*eth*
custom	*mor*
to cut	*-cide, cis*
to cut	*cop*
to cut	*coup*
to cut	*sect, sec*
to cut	*shear, shor*
to cut	*tail*
to cut	*tom, tme*
to cut	*tons*
to cut	*trench, trunc*
Cyprus	*cypr*

D

to damage	*lid, lis*
to dance	*chor*
to dance	*orch*
dark	*amaur*
dark	*fusc*
dark	*maur*
darkness	*scot*
daughter of	*-ovna*
dawn	*eo-*
day	*day*
day	*dia*
day	*hemer*
day	*journ*

dead	*necr, nec*
dear	*car*
dear	*lef*
death	*bane*
death	*leth*
death	*mort*
death	*necr, nec*
death	*thanat, than*
decay	*cari*
to deceive	*fall, fals*
to declare	*say*
to decorate	*orn*
deep	*bath*
deer	*elaph*
to define	*hor*
delta-shaped (△)	*delt*
demon	*demon*
dense	*das*
to deny	*neg*
depth	*byss, byth*
descendant of	*-ek, -ik*
descendant of	*-ez*
to desire	*av*
to desire	*cup*
to desire	*desider*
to destroy	*del*
devil	*cobalt*
devil	*diabol*
devil	*nickel*
to devour	*vor*
to die	*star*

to dig	*grav*
to digest	*pept, peps*
dinner	*deipn*
to dip	*bapt*
to dip	*merg, mers*
direction whence	*-erly*
disease	*morb*
disease	*nos*
disease	*path*
dish	*patell*
disk	*disc*
disturb	*stir*
ditch	*foss*
diverse	*var*
to divide	*shear, shor*
divination	*-mancy*
to do	*ag, ig, act*
to do	*-ate*
to do	*don*
to do	*dra*
to do	*fac, fic, fect, -fy*
to do	*-ize, -ise*
to do	*pract, prax*
dog	*can, cyn*
doll	*cor*
doll	*pup*
dolphin	*delph*
something done	*-em*
something done	*-eme*
something done	*-ma*
something done	*-men*

something done	-y
door	for
door	osti
(folding) door	valv
doorway	jan
doorway	port
double	diplo-
dough	past
dove	columb
down	cata-, cath-, cat-
down	de-
to drag	tract
to draw	drag
to draw	tract
dress	vest
to drink	bib
to drink	drink
to drink	pot, pos
to drip	drip
dripping	stalagm, stalact
to drive	ag, ig, act
to drive	drif
a drop	gutt
a drop	stil
drug	pharmac
drum	tympan
dry	arid
dry	dryg
dry	scel
dry	sicc, sec
dry	xer

dull	*ambly*
dull	*hebet*
struck dumb	*stup*
dung	*copr*
dung	*guan*
dung	*scat, skat*
dung	*sterc*
dust	*coni, koni*
dust	*pulver*
dwarf	*nan*
to dye	*ting, tinct*

E

eagle	*aquil*
ear	*aur*
ear	*ot*
eardrum	*myring*
early	*eo-*
to earn	*mer*
earth	*chamae*
earth	*chthon*
earth	*ge*
earth	*tellur*
earth	*terr*
ease	*oti*
east	*anatol*
east	*euro-*
east	*orient*
to eat	*phag*
to eat	*vor*

egg	*oö-*
egg	*ov*
eight	*octo-, oct-*
elbow	*uln*
electric	*electr*
suffix from "electron"	*-tron*
chemical element	*-ium*
empty	*cen*
empty	*jejun*
empty	*vac*
empty	*van*
enclosure	*cohort*
enclosure	*geard*
enclosure	*phragm, phrax*
enclosure	*sty*
end	*fin*
end	*tele, teli, telo*
end	*termin, term*
English	*angl*
full enjoyment	*fruct*
to enliven	*veg*
enough	*sat*
to entice	*lic*
entirely	*tot*
to entrust	*mand*
equal	*equ*
equal	*iso-*
equal	*par*
to establish	*fund, found*
evening	*hesper*
everywhere	*ubiqu*

to examine	*skep*
to excavate	*dig*
to excite	*hormon*
to extend	*strec*
extremity	*acro*
extremity	*apic*
eye	*ocul*
eye	*omma, ommat*
eye	*op*
eye	*ophthalm*
eyelash	*cili*
eyelid	*blephar*
eyelid	*cili*
(edge of) eyelid	*tars*

F

face	*fac*
face	*prosop*
faith	*fid*
faithful	*tru*
to fall	*cad, cid, cas*
to fall	*pto*
falling	*caduc*
falling	*occident*
false	*pseud*
false	*spuri*
fame	*ro*
farmer	*bor*
farmer	*georg*
to fashion	*fig*

fast	*celer*
fast	*tach*
fast	*veloc*
to fasten	*fix*
to fasten	*pact*
to fasten	*pec, pex, pag*
fasting	*jejun*
fat	*adip*
fat	*lip, lipo-*
fat	*seb*
fat	*steat, stear*
father	*pap, pop*
father	*pater*
fault	*culp*
fault	*mend*
favor	*charis*
to fear	*phob*
to fear	*tim*
feast	*fest*
feather	*pinn, pinnat, penn*
feather	*plum*
feather	*pter*
feathered	*fledge*
to feed	*fed*
to feed	*past*
to feel	*sens, sent*
feeler	*palp*
feeling	*esthet, esthes*
feeling	*path*
female	*femin*
female	*wif*

feminine	*-a*
feminine	*-ess*
feminine	*-rix, -trix*
fence	*phragm, phrax*
to ferment	*brew*
ferment	*zym*
fern	*pterid*
fervor	*zeal*
fever	*febr*
fever	*pyret*
few	*oligo-*
few	*pauci-*
fiber	*fibr*
fiber	*in*
field	*agr*
field	*camp*
to fight	*-machy*
to fight	*milit*
to fight	*pugn*
figure	*schemat*
to filter	*col*
filthy	*ful*
fin	*branchi*
to find	*heur*
finger	*dactyl*
finger	*digit*
fire	*ign*
fire	*pyr*
first	*arch*
first	*prim, prin*
first	*proto-*

fish	*ichthy*
fish	*pisc*
to fit	*apt, ept*
fitting	*met*
five	*penta-*
five	*quinqu-, quint-*
flame	*flam*
flame	*phlegm*
flame	*phlog*
flank	*lapar*
flask	*ampull*
flat	*plac*
flat	*plan*
flat	*platy-*
flat cake	*placent*
flat ground	*sol*
flax	*byss*
flax	*lin*
to flee	*fug*
Flemish	*flem, flam*
flesh	*carn*
flesh	*creat-, cre-, kre-*
flesh	*sarc*
to flick	*whisk*
flint	*silic*
to float	*flot*
flock	*greg*
flour	*aleur*
flour	*far*
to flow	*flu, flux*
to flow	*-rrhage, -rrhex*

to flow	*-rrhea*
flower	*anth*
flower	*flor*
flower (name)	*-ia*
to fluctuate	*oscill*
fluid	*chyl*
fluid	*chym*
fluid	*liqu*
flute	*aul*
flute	*tibi*
a fly	*musc*
foam	*aphr*
focus	*foc*
fog	*typh*
-fold	*-fold*
-fold	*-ple*
to fold	*plex, plic, ply*
to follow	*sequ, sec*
food	*met*
food	*sit, siti*
foolish	*fatu*
foot	*fot, fet*
foot	*ped*
foot	*pod, pus*
footprint	*vestig*
for	*pro-*
(river) ford	*-ford*
forehead	*front*
foreign	*barbar*
foreign	*wal*
foreign	*xen*

forest	*silv, sylv*
to forget	*leth*
to forget	*obliv*
fork	*furc*
form	*eido-*
form	*form*
form	*morph*
to form	*plas*
form	*schemat*
form	*shape*
fort	*-burg, -burgh*
fort	*-bury, -borough*
fort	*-caster, -cester*
forward	*pro-*
forward	*pros-*
foul matter	*pur, pus*
four	*quadr-, quart*
four	*tetra*
fox	*vulp*
French	*franc*
French	*gall*
free	*eleuther*
free	*franc*
free	*grat*
free	*liber*
to free	*lys, lyt*
to free	*solv, solu*
freeman	*carl*
to frighten	*terr*
fringe	*fimbr*
frog	*ran*

rom	*ab-*
rom	*apo-, ap-*
rom	*cata-, cath-, cat-*
rom	*de-*
rom	*dis-, di-, dif-*
rom	*e-, ex-*
om	*ec-*
ont	*anter-*
ont	*pros-*
ost	*crym*
ost	*gel*
uit	*carp*
uit	*fruct*
uit	*pom*
uit-stone	*pyren*
ll	*plen, plet, -ply*
ll	*pleth*
ngus	*agaric*
ngus	*myc*
nnel	*choan*
rrow	*sulc*

ll	*bil*
ll	*chol*
p	*hiat*
rden	*cohort*
rden	*geard*
s	*man*
te	*port*

gate	*pyl*
to gather	*leg, lig, lect*
German	*german*
to get	*get*
giant	*gigant*
gift	*dor*
gift	*mun*
gill	*branchi*
girdle	*cest*
girdle	*cinct*
girdle	*zon*
to give	*don, dat*
to give	*dos, dot*
to give	*gif*
gland	*aden*
gland	*balan*
glass	*hyal*
glass	*vitr*
to glide	*slip*
glowing	*cand*
glue	*coll*
glue	*gli*
glue	*glutin*
to gnaw	*rode, ros*
to go	*bas, bat, bet*
to go	*cede, ceed, cess*
to go	*fare*
to go	*it*
to go	*vad, vas*
to go up	*sti*
goat	*aeg*

goat	*capr*
goat	*trag*
God	*dei, div*
God	*god*
God	*the, theo*
God's gracious gift	*joan, john*
gold	*aur*
gold	*chrys*
good	*agath*
good	*bene-*
good	*bon*
good	*eu-*
good	*prob*
goose	*anser*
goose	*chen*
goose	*gos*
grain	*chondr*
grain	*far*
grain	*gran*
grain	*sit, siti*
grainy	*granat*
grandson of	*o'*
grape	*acin*
little grape	*uvul*
bunch of grapes	*staphyl*
grapevine	*vit*
grass	*gramin*
grass	*herb*
gratitude	*charis*
gray	*cani*
gray	*poli*

gray-green	*glauc*
to graze	*bosc, bot*
great	*grand*
great	*macro-*
great	*magn-*
great	*maha-*
great	*mega-, megal-, meg-*
greater	*magister*
greater	*major*
greatest	*maxim*
Greek ending	*-on*
Greek plural ending	*-a*
green	*chlor*
green	*pras*
green	*virid*
gridiron	*rost*
grief	*dol*
to grieve	*murn*
to grind	*mael*
to grind (grain)	*mol*
gristle	*cartilag*
groin	*ile*
groin	*ili*
ground	*edaph*
ground	*hum*
ground	*ped*
group	*-ad*
group	*-ida*
group	*-ome*
to grow	*cresc, crease, cret, cru*

to grow	*grow*
growth	*-oma*
growth	*phym*
guard	*custod*
guard	*phylac*
to guard	*tu*
to guide	*tech*
gums	*gingiv*
gums	*ul*

H

hailstone	*chalaz*
hair	*capill*
hair	*com*
hair	*crin*
hair	*pil*
hair	*trich, thrix*
half	*demi-*
half	*hemi-*
half	*med*
half	*mezz*
half	*semi-*
hammer	*malle*
hand	*chir, cheir*
hand	*manu*
handle	*ans*
to hang	*aort*
to hang	*hang*
to hang	*pend, pens*
to hang over	*min*

to happen	*cad, cid, cas*
happy	*felic*
harbor	*port*
hard	*dur*
hard	*hard, -ard*
hard	*scirrh*
hard	*scler*
harmony	*cosm*
harmony	*cosmet*
harrow	*hears*
hatchet	*pelecy*
to hate	*mis-*
to hate	*odi*
to have	*hab*
to have	*hav*
to have	*own*
head	*capit*
head	*cephal*
back of head	*occip*
head	*poll*
headband	*mitr*
healing	*iatr*
health	*hygi*
health	*salut*
healthy	*hal*
healthy	*hol*
healthy	*san*
to be healthy	*val*
heap	*cumul*
heap	*mol*
to hear	*acou, acu*

o hear	*audi*
o hear	*her*
heart	*card*
heart	*cord*
heart	*heart*
heat	*therm*
heaven	*cel*
heavenly	*-lani*
heavens	*uran*
heavy	*grav*
o heed	*reck*
eel	*calc*
eir	*her, hered*
Hermes	*herm*
ernia	*-cele*
idden	*calypt*
idden	*crypt, krypt*
lie hidden	*lanthan, lat*
hide	*cell*
hide	*cond*
hide	*cover*
hide	*hel*
gh	*acro*
gh	*alt*
gh	*haut*
gh	*hyps*
ghest point	*summ*
ll	*mount, mont*
p	*cox*
p	*ischi*

hip	*sciat*
to hold	*hald*
to hold	*hec, hex, ech*
to hold	*ten, tin, tain*
hole	*hol*
hole	*tremat*
hollow	*can*
hollow	*cav*
hollow	*coel, cel*
hollow	*colp*
hollow	*lacun*
hollow	*scaph*
hollow	*sinus, sinu*
holy	*hagi*
holy	*hal*
holy	*pi*
holy	*sacr*
holy	*san, sant*
holy	*sanct*
home	*dom*
home	*eco-, oec*
home	*ham, -heim, home*
honey	*mell*
honeycomb	*fav*
honor	*tim*
honored	*sebast*
hoof	*chel*
hoof	*ungul*
hook	*croc*
hook	*onc*
to hope	*sper*

horn	corn
horn	kerat, cerat
horse	caval
horse	equ
horse	hipp
hot	cal
hour	hor
house	cas
house	hus, hous
human being	anthrop
human being	homo
human being	man
humpbacked	kyph
hundred	cent
hundred	hecto-, hecato-
husband	marit

I

I	ego
ice	glac
idea	ideo-
ileum	ile
ilium	ili
image	icon
image	idol
to imitate	mim
to impel	cit
impression	typ
in	a-

in	*en-, em-*
in	*in-, im-, il-, ir-*
incense	*thur*
to increase	*aug*
to increase	*aux*
Indian	*ind*
inferior	*-aster*
inflammation	*-itis*
information about	*-ana*
-ing	*-ant*
-ing	*-end, -and*
-ing	*-ent*
-ing	*-ion, -tion*
to inhabit	*col, cult*
to injure	*noc, nox*
insanity	*mania*
insect	*entom*
inside	*endo-*
inside	*int-*
inside	*intro-, intra-*
instep	*tars*
instrument	*organ*
intensive	*be-*
intensive	*com-, co-, col-, con-, cor-*
intensive	*en-, em-*
intensive	*per-, pel-*
internal organs	*viscer*
to interpret	*red*
large intestine	*col*
intestine	*enter*
into	*en-, em-*

into	*in-, im-, il-, ir-*
iris (of eye)	*irid*
Irish	*hibern*
iron	*ferr*
iron	*sider*
island	*insul*
island	*nes*
Italian	*ital*
itch	*psor*
ivory	*eburn*

J

jackass	*asin*
jaw	*gnath*
lower jaw	*mandib*
jaw	*maxill*
Jewish	*jud*
to join	*junct, jug, join*
joined	*zyg, zeug*
joint	*arthr, art*
joint	*vertebr*
joke	*joc*
Jove (Jupiter)	*jov*
to judge	*cri*
to judge	*dem*
judge	*jud*
judgment	*sap*
juice	*chyl*
juice	*chym*
to jump	*sal, sil, sult*

K

Kadmos (Greek hero)	*cadm*
kernel	*nucle*
key	*clav*
key	*cleid, cleis*
kidney	*nephr*
kidney	*ren*
to kill	*-cide, cis*
kind	*gen*
what kind	*qual*
king	*basil*
king	*reg*
knee	*gen, gon*
knife	*cutl*
knot	*gangli*
to knot	*nect*
knot	*nod*
to know (how)	*can, con, ken*
to know	*cogn*
to know	*gnos, gnom*
to know	*know*
to know	*no*
to know	*sci*
to know	*wit, wis*
knuckle	*condyl*

L

L	*lambd*
to lack	*lip*

to lack	*-penia*
ladder	*climac*
ladder	*scala*
lady	*dam*
lambda (λ, Λ)	*lambd*
lame	*claud*
to lament	*plain*
language	*gloss, glot*
language	*lingu*
larger	*major*
largest	*maxim*
larva	*larv*
last	*eschat*
last	*fin*
last	*ultim*
lasting	*dur*
late	*opsi-*
late	*tard*
Latin ending	*-a*
Latin ending	*-um*
Latin ending	*-us*
Latin plural ending	*-a*
Latin plural ending	*-ae*
Latin plural ending	*-i*
lattice	*cancel*
to laugh	*gel, gelot*
to laugh	*rid, ris*
law	*leg*
law	*nom*
to lay	*leg*
layer	*lamin, lamell*

to lead	*duc*
to lead	*led*
to lead	*men*
lead (metal)	*molybd*
lead (metal)	*plumb*
leader	*agog*
leaf	*foli*
leaf	*lamin, lamell*
leaf	*petal*
leaf	*phyll*
to lean	*clin, climat*
to lean	*verg*
to leap	*leap*
to leap	*sal, sil, sult*
to learn	*math*
least	*minim*
leather	*cor*
to leave	*linqu, lict*
to leave	*lip*
left hand	*levo-, laevo-*
left hand	*sinistr*
leg	*crur*
leg	*scel*
leisure	*oti*
leisure	*schol*
lens	*phac, phak*
lentil	*lent*
lentil	*phac, phak*
less	*mi*
less	*min*
letter	*liter*

lid	*opercul*
to lie (down)	*cumb, cub*
to lie	*pseud*
to lie open	*pat, pass*
life	*anima*
life	*bio*
life	*lif*
life	*spir*
life	*vita*
life	*-zoic*
to lift	*aort*
to lift	*hev*
ligament	*des, dem*
light (in weight)	*elaphr*
light (in weight)	*lev*
light	*liht*
light	*luc*
light	*lumin*
light	*phot, phos*
lightning	*ceraun, keraun*
like	*-al*
like	*-an*
like	*-ane*
like	*-ar*
like	*-ary*
like	*-cund, -und*
like	*-ent*
like	*-eous*
like	*-ese*
like	*-ic*
like	*-ical*

like	-id
like	-ile
like	-ine
like	-ish
like	lik
like	-ory
like	simil
lily	crin
limb	mel
limb	membr
lime	calc
limit	fin
line	line
line	stich
linen	byss
lion	leon
lip	cheil, chil
lip	labi, labr
liquid	hum
(watery) liquid	ser
little	-cle, -cule
little	-ek, -ik
little	-el
little	-ette, -et
little	-kin
little	lept
little	-let
little	-ling
little	micro-
little	min
little	-ock

little	*parv*
little	*paul*
little	*petit*
little	*-ule, -ula*
little	*-y, -ie*
to live	*bio*
to live	*lif*
to live	*viv*
lively	*vig*
liver	*hepat*
lizard	*saur*
to load	*charg*
loaf (bread)	*laf*
lobe	*lob*
loin	*lumb*
long	*dolicho-*
long	*long*
to look	*blep*
to look	*spec, spic*
to look	*scop*
to look at	*-orama*
to look at	*show*
to look at	*skep*
to look at	*the*
to look at	*tu*
loose	*lack*
loose	*lax*
loose	*leas, laiss*
to loose	*lys, lyt*
to loose	*solv, solu*
to lose	*los*

loss	*damn*
lot	*cler*
lot	*sort*
louse	*pedicul*
love	*agap*
to love	*am*
to love	*ero*
to love	*fre*
to love	*phil*
low	*bass*
low	*chamae*
lump	*chalaz*
lung	*pneumon, pneum, pne*
lung	*pulm, pulmon*
lust	*-lagnia*

M

machine	*mechan*
Magnesia (in Thessaly)	*magnes, magnet*
maiden	*nymph*
to make	*-ate*
to make	*be-*
to make	*creat*
to make	*-en*
to make	*fac, fic, fect, -fy*
to make	*-ize, -ise*
to make	*mak*
to make	*poie, poe*
to make certain	*cern, cert*

man	*andr*
man	*anthrop*
man	*carl*
man	*homo*
man	*man*
man	*mascul*
man	*vir*
manly	*arsen*
manner	*mod*
in the manner of	*-atim*
in the manner of	*-esque*
in the manner of	*-ly*
in the manner of	*-wise*
mantle	*palli*
mantle	*tunic*
many	*multi-*
many	*myria-*
many	*poly-*
how many	*quot*
mark	*macul*
mark	*stib*
to mark	*stig, sting, stinct*
marketplace	*agor*
marriage	*gam*
marrow	*medull*
marrow	*myel*
to marry	*junct, jug, join*
to marry	*nub, nupt*
Mars (Ares)	*areo*
Mars	*mar*
mask	*larv*

Mass (ceremony)	*-mas*
mass	*onc*
master	*domin*
mating	*gam*
mating	*junct, jug, join*
matter	*hyl, yl*
mature	*fledge*
mature	*pub*
maze	*labyrinth*
meadow	*-ley*
meaning	*sem*
to measure	*mens*
to measure	*met*
measure	*meter, metr*
measure	*mod*
measured flow	*rhythm*
meat	*carn*
meat	*creat, cre-, kre-*
meat	*met*
meat	*sarc*
to meet	*met*
member	*membr*
fetal membrane	*chori*
membrane	*hymen*
membrane	*mening*
membrane	*myring*
Mercury	*mercur*
merry	*hilar*
message	*angel*
messenger	*angel*
metal plate	*elasm*

middle	*med*
middle	*meso-*
middle	*mezz-*
Milan (Italy)	*milan*
mild	*leni*
mildew	*mucedin*
milk	*galact*
milk	*lac*
million	*mega-, megal-, meg-*
mind	*ment*
mind	*psych*
miracle	*thaum*
mite	*acar*
to mix	*misc*
to mix	*mix*
to mix	*mong*
mixing	*cras*
proper mixture	*temper*
mob	*demo-*
mob	*ochlo-*
mob	*pleb*
mob	*vulg*
model	*typ*
to be modest	*pud*
mold	*eurot*
moldy	*muc*
money	*fe*
money	*lucr*
money	*pecu*
monster	*terat*
month	*men*

month	*mens*
month	*-mester*
moon	*lun*
moon	*men*
moon	*mens*
moon	*mon*
moon	*selen*
more	*-er*
more	*ple, plei*
more	*plus, plur*
moss	*bry*
most	*-est*
mother	*mater*
mother	*metr*
mountain	*-berg*
mountain	*mount, mont*
mouse	*mus*
mouse	*my*
mouth	*bucc*
mouth (of river)	*-mouth*
mouth	*or, os*
mouth	*stom*
to move	*kine-, cinema-*
to move	*mov, mot, mob*
how much	*quant*
mucus	*blenn*
mucus	*muc*
mucus	*myx*
muscle	*mus*
muscle	*my*
Muse	*mus*

mussel	*mytil*
to mutilate	*maym*
mutually	*allel*
my	*mon-, ma-*
mystery	*myst*

<u>N</u>

nail	*clav*
(finger-)nail	*onych*
naked	*gym*
naked	*nud*
name	*nam*
name	*nomin, nom*
name	*onym, onoma*
narrow	*angust*
narrow	*sten*
nation	*ethn*
nation	*gen*
natural	*physi*
nature	*physi*
navel	*omphal*
navel	*umbilic*
near	*engy-*
near	*neigh*
near	*prox*
neck	*cervic*
neck	*coll*
neck	*trachel*
need	*ned*
to need	*-penia*
negative	*a-, an-*

negative	*de-*
negative	*dis-, di-, dif-*
negative	*in-, il-, im-, ir-*
negative	*n-*
negative	*ne-*
negative	*non-*
negative	*un-*
neighbor	*vicin*
neither	*neutr*
nephew	*nepot*
Neptune	*neptun*
nerve	*nerv*
nerve	*neur*
nest	*nid*
net	*dicty, dikty*
net	*ret*
nettle	*cnid*
new	*cen, caen, -cene*
new	*neo-*
new	*nov*
next to	*juxta-*
nickel	*nickel*
night	*niht*
night	*noc, nox*
night	*nyct*
nine	*ennea-*
nine	*novem, non*
nipple	*papill*
nipple	*thel*
niter	*nitr*
nitrogen	*nitr*

(dull) noise	*bomb*
noon	*meridi*
no-place	*utop*
north	*arct*
north	*boreal*
north	*hyperbor*
north	*nor-*
north	*septentrion*
nose	*nas, nar*
nose	*nos*
nose	*rhin*
not	*a-, an-*
not	*de-*
not	*dis-, di-, dif-*
not	*in-, il-, im-, ir-*
not	*n-*
not	*ne-*
not	*non-*
not	*un-*
notch	*scor*
nothing	*nul, nihil*
to nourish	*al*
to nourish	*nutri*
to nourish	*troph*
nucleus	*kary, cary*
numb	*torp*
number	*arithm*
number	*numer*
numbness	*narc*
nut	*kary, cary*
nut	*nucle*

_O_

oak	*rob*
oar	*rem*
oblique	*lox*
oblique	*obliqu*
oblique	*plagi*
petty obstacle	*tric*
to obstruct	*cumber*
obstruction	*barr*
offspring	*prol*
oil	*ole, -ol*
to oil	*unct, oint*
old	*ger*
old	*presby*
old	*sen*
old	*vet*
(Mt.) Olympus	*olymp*
on	*a-*
on	*epi-, ep-*
one	*hen*
one	*mono-*
one	*uni-*
one-and-one-half	*sesqui-*
one who	*-aire, -air*
one who	*-an, -ian*
one who	*-ant*
one who	*-ar*
one who	*-ard, -art*
one who	*-ary*
one who	*-ast*

one who	*-ate*
one who (passive)	*-ee*
one who	*-eer*
one who	*-ent*
one who	*-er, -yer*
one who	*-ero*
one who	*-eur*
one who	*-ier*
one who	*-ist*
one who	*-ite*
one who	*-ive*
one who	*-nik*
one who	*-or*
one who	*-ster*
to open	*apert*
opening	*chasm*
opening	*for*
opening	*foramin*
opening	*lumin*
opening	*osti*
opening	*por*
opening	*stom*
opening	*trema*
opinion	*dog, dox*
opium	*opi*
opposite	*anti-, ant-*
opposite	*contra-, counter-*
orange	*fulv*
orange	*rutil*
order	*nom*
order	*ordin*

other	*all*
other	*alter, al*
other	*hetero-*
out	*ab-*
out	*apo-, ap-*
out	*cata-, cath-, cat-*
out	*de-*
out	*dis-, di-, dif-*
out	*e-, ex-*
out	*ec-*
out	*out-*
out	*ut*
outdoors	*for*
outer	*ecto-*
outside	*ecto-*
outside	*epi-, ep-*
outside	*exo-*
outside	*exter-*
outside	*extra-*
outward	*extra-*
over	*hyper-*
over	*super-, supra-, sur-*
to owe	*deb*
one's own	*idio-*
one's own	*propr*
ox	*bou, bov*

P

| pain | *alg* |
| pain | *odyn* |

painful	*sor*
to paint	*pict*
paired	*zyg, zeug*
pale	*blanc*
pale	*bleach*
pale	*ochr*
pale	*pal*
Pallas	*pallad*
pan	*patell*
paper	*cart*
paralysis	*pleg*
part	*deal*
part	*mer*
part	*part*
passage	*por*
to pat	*palp*
path	*path*
pause	*paul*
pause	*paus*
to pay	*pend, pens*
peace	*pac*
pear	*pyr*
pearl	*margarit*
peasant	*bor*
pebble	*calcul*
pen	*styl*
penis	*balan*
penis	*pen*
penis	*phall*
people	*demo*
people	*folk*

people	*la*
people	*ochlo-*
people	*pleb*
people	*popul*
people	*vulg*
to perceive	*cern, cert*
perforated	*ethm*
perforation	*cente*
to perform	*funct*
permissible	*lic*
Persian	*persic*
personal	*idio-*
personal	*propr*
to persuade	*suad, suas*
phlegm	*pituit*
phylum	*phyl*
to pierce	*broc*
to pierce	*stik*
to pierce	*thrill*
pigeon	*columb*
pillar	*cion*
pin	*fibul*
pinecone	*pin*
pinecone	*strobil*
pipe	*aul*
pipe	*solen*
pipe	*syring*
pipe	*tub*
pit	*alveol*
place	*loc*
to place	*pon, pos*

place	*stall*
place	*stead*
to place	*thes, thet*
place	*top*
place where	*-ary, -arium*
place where	*-ery*
place where	*-ory, -orium*
plague	*pest*
plank	*tabl*
plant	*phyt*
thin plate	*petal*
platinum	*platin*
to play	*lud, lus*
to please	*plac*
pleased	*grat*
pleasure	*hedon*
to pledge	*spond, spons*
plowshare	*vomer*
to pluck	*tes*
plumb-line	*plumb*
to plunge	*merg, mers*
Pluto	*plut*
point	*cuspid*
pointer	*indic*
poison	*tox*
poison	*venen*
poison	*vir*
to polish	*pol*
Polish	*pol*
pollution	*miasm*
pollution	*mys*

pool	*limn*
pool	*stagn*
poplar	*alam*
portion	*cler*
potash	*potass*
potassium	*potass*
to pound	*tus*
to pour	*chem*
to pour	*fus, fund, found*
power	*dyn, dynam*
power	*erg, urg*
having the power of	*-ive*
pox	*variol*
praise	*dog, dox*
to pray	*bid, bead*
to pray	*ora*
to pray	*prec*
precious	*dear*
to prepare	*par*
to press	*press, print*
to press together	*arct*
to press together	*stip*
pressure	*bar*
to prevent	*para*
price	*preci*
to prick	*pung, punct*
to prick	*stig, sting, stinct*
to proclaim	*ban*
to produce	*poie, poe*
profit	*lucr*
to project	*min*

projecting	*glochi*
Prometheus	*prometh*
proper	*dec*
property	*fe*
property	*pecu*
prostitute	*porn*
to protect	*alex*
to protect	*gar*
to protect	*ward*
to protect	*warn*
provident	*prometh*
prow	*rostr*
to prune	*put*
pubic	*pub*
pug-nosed	*sim*
to pull	*tract*
pulley	*troch*
pulse	*sphygm*
puncture	*cente*
puncture	*nyx*
puncture	*pung, punct*
to punish	*pun*
punishment	*pen*
pupil (eye)	*cor*
pure	*cast*
pure	*cath, kath*
purple	*purpur*
to pursue	*hunt*
pus	*py*
to push	*pel, puls*
to push	*shuf*

pushing	*osm*
to put	*pon, pos*
to put	*thes, thet*
putrid	*sapr*
putrid	*seps, sept*
puzzle	*enigm*

Q

having the quality of	*-aceous*
having the quality of	*-acious*
quality	*-acity*
quality	*-acy, -cy*
quality	*-age*
quality	*-ance*
quality	*-ancy*
quality	*-aneity, -eity*
having the quality of	*-aneous*
quality	*-asia, -asis*
quality	*-asm*
having the quality of	*-ate*
quality	*-dom*
having the quality of	*-en*
quality	*-ence*
quality	*-ency*
having the quality of	*-eous*
quality	*-ery, -ry*
quality	*-esis*
quality	*-ety*
having the quality of	*-ful*

quality	-hood
quality	-ion, -tion
quality	-ism
having the quality of	-ite
having the quality of	-itious
quality	-ity
having the quality of	-ly
quality	-ment
quality	-mony
quality	-ness
having the quality of	-orious
having the quality of	-ory
having the quality of	-ose
having the quality of	-otic
having the quality of	-ous
having the quality of	-ow
quality	-ship
quality	-th
quality	-tude
quality	-ty
having the quality of	-ulent
having the quality of	-ulous
having the quality of	-uous
quality	-ure
quality	-y
having the quality of	-y

R

| rabies | rab |
| race | ethn |

race	*gen*
race	*phyl*
rain	*hyet*
rain	*ombr*
rain	*pluvi*
rainbow	*irid*
to raise	*lev*
to raise	*tol*
a ram	*cri*
in ranks	*phalang*
raven	*corac*
ray	*actin*
ray	*rad*
to read	*leg, lig, lect*
to read	*-lexia*
to reason	*rat*
recent	*cen, caen, -cene*
to recite	*spell*
to reckon	*rat*
red	*erythr*
red	*phoenic*
red	*red*
red	*rhod*
red	*ros*
red	*rub*
red	*ruf*
red	*rutil*
reed	*calam*
reed	*can*
to relate	*tell, tal*
related to	*-ac, -iac*

related to	-al
related to	-an
related to	-ane
related to	-ar
related to	-ary
related to	-cund, -und
related to	-ent
related to	-eous
related to	-ern
related to	-ese
related to	-ic
related to	-ical
related to	-id
related to	-ile
related to	-ine
related to	-ish
related to	-ite
related to	-otic
relative	sib
to remember	memor
to remember	mne
to remind	moni
reproductive	gono-
resemblance	eido-
resembling	-oid, -oda, -ode
to rest	quies, quiet
result	-em
result	-eme
result	-ma
result	-men

result	-y
a revel	com
Rhine	rhen
rib	cost
rib	pleur
ribbon	taen
to ride	rid
right	orth-
right	rect
right	reg
right hand	dextr
rind	lemm
ring	an
ring	annel, annul
ring	cortic
ring	cric
ring	gyr
ring	sphincter
ripe	ripe
to rise	ori, ort
to rise	ris
rising	orient
river	guad
river	potam
road	od, hod
road	via
to rob	rob, rev
rock	lapid
rock	-lite
rock	lith
rock	petr

rock	*sax*
rock	*ston, stan*
rod	*can*
rod	*rhabd*
to roll	*roll, rol*
to roll	*volv, volu*
Roman	*roman*
roof	*steg*
room	*cell*
root	*radic*
root	*rhiz*
rope	*fun*
rose	*ros*
rotten	*putr*
rough	*asper*
rough	*trachy*
round	*circul*
royal	*basil*
royal	*reg*
to rub	*fric*
to rub	*trip, trib*
to rub	*trit*
to rule	*arch*
a rule	*can*
to rule	*-crat, crac*
a rule	*norm*
to rule	*rect*
to rule	*reg*
rump	*glute*
rump	*pyg*
to run	*cur, course*

to run	*drom*
to run	*leap*
to run	*run*
runner	*trochanter*
Russia	*russ*
Russia	*ruthen*

S

S	*sigm*
sack	*burs*
sack	*pock*
sacred	*hier*
sacred	*sacr*
safe	*salv*
safety	*soter*
to sail	*naut*
to sail	*nav*
saint	*san, sant*
saliva	*ptyal*
saliva	*sial*
a salt	*hal*
salt	*sal*
salvation	*soter*
same	*homo-*
same	*ident*
same	*tauto-*
sand	*aren*
Sardinia	*sardin*
Saturn	*saturn*
sausage	*botul*

a saw	serrat, serr
(made by Adolphe) Sax	sax
Saxons	-sex
to say	dict
to say	phe, phas
scale	lep, lepid
scale	squam
Scandinavia	scand
scar	ul
science	-ics
to scrape	ras, rad
to scrape	scrap
to scream	gal
sea	mar
sea	pelag
sea	thalass, thalatt
seal	bull
seal (animal)	phoc
seashore	littor
seat	hedr
second	deuter
to see	blep
to see	id, eid
to see	op
to see	-orama
to see	scop
to see	see
to see	spec, spic
to see	vid, vis
seed	semin
seed	sperm

seed	*spor*
to seek	*petit*
to seek	*quest, quir, quis*
to seem	*think*
to seize	*cap, cip, cept, ceive*
to seize	*empt*
to seize	*grip*
to seize	*hunt*
to seize	*lab, lept*
to seize	*prehend, prehens, pris*
to seize	*sum, sumpt*
to seize	*rap*
seizure	*agra*
self	*auto-*
self	*ego*
self	*sui*
to sell	*poly*
to sell	*sell*
to sell	*vend*
to send	*mit, miss*
to send	*stol, stal, -stle*
to separate	*crin*
separate	*priv*
separated	*chorist*
series	*ser*
serious	*sever*
to serve	*minister*
to serve	*serv*
service	*mun*
(stage-) set	*scen*
to set	*sist*

to set	*sit, set*
to set	*sta, stit*
to set up	*stor*
seven	*hept-*
seven	*sept-*
to sew	*raph, raphid, -rrhaph*
sewer	*cloac*
sexual	*vener*
shade	*shad*
shade	*umbr*
shadow	*sci, ski*
shaggy	*rugh*
shaggy	*vill*
to shake	*seism*
to shake	*shake*
to shake	*trem, trom*
shank	*crur*
shape	*form*
shape	*morph*
to share	*trib*
sharp	*ac, acr*
sharp	*oxy*
to shear	*tons*
sheath	*cole*
sheath	*vagin*
sheet	*lamin, lamell*
small sheet	*nap*
shell	*cochl*
shell	*conch*
shell	*ostrac*
shelter	*burg*

shield	*aspid*
shield	*clype*
shield	*scut*
shield	*thyr*
shinbone	*cnem*
shinbone	*tibi*
to shine	*shin*
to shine	*splend*
ship	*nav*
shoe	*calce*
to shoot	*shot*
short	*brachy-*
short	*brev*
shoulder-blade	*scapul*
to shout	*clam, claim*
to show	*phan, phen*
to show	*tech*
sickle	*falc*
side	*cost*
side	*hedr*
side	*later*
side	*pleur*
side	*side*
sieve	*ethm*
sight	*op*
sigma-shaped (S)	*sigm*
sign	*beck*
sign	*mark*
sign	*sem*
sign	*sign*
silent	*tac, tic*

silicon	*silic*
silk	*seric*
silver	*argent*
silver	*argyr*
silver	*platin*
similar	*lik*
to sing	*gal*
to sing	*sing*
single	*haplo-*
single	*mono-*
single	*priv*
single	*uni-*
sinus	*antr*
sinus	*sinus, sinu*
sister	*soror*
to sit	*sed, sid, sess*
to sit	*sit, set*
six	*hexa-*
six	*sex-*
skill	*art*
skill	*techn*
skin	*chori*
skin	*cut*
skin	*derm*
skin	*lemm*
skin	*pel*
skull	*crani*
sky	*cel*
sky	*uran*
slave	*thrall*
Slavic	*slav*

to slay	*sla*
to sleep	*com*
to sleep	*dorm*
sleep	*hypn*
sleep	*somn*
to slide	*slid*
to slip	*lapse*
slippery	*lubr*
slope	*clin, climat*
slow	*brady-*
slow	*lent*
slow	*slow*
slow	*tard*
small	*-cle, -cule*
small	*-ek, -ik*
small	*-el*
small	*-ette, -et*
small	*-kin*
small	*lept*
small	*-let*
small	*-ling*
small	*micro-*
small	*min*
small	*-ock*
small	*parv*
small	*paul*
small	*petit*
small	*-ule, -ula*
small	*-y, -ie*
smallest	*minim*
smell	*od*

smell	*osm*
smell	*osphr*
smelling	*olfact*
smoke	*capn*
smoke	*fum*
smooth	*leio-, lio*
smooth	*lev*
snake	*angui*
snake	*colubr*
snake	*herpet*
snake	*ophi, ophidi*
to snare	*lic*
to snatch	*rap*
snout	*rhynch*
snow	*chion, chio*
snow	*niv*
snub-nosed	*sim*
soap	*sap*
soda	*sod*
sodium	*sod*
soft	*leni*
soft	*malac*
soft	*moll*
soft (sound)	*plan*
sole (of foot)	*plant*
solid	*solid*
solid	*stereo-, ster*
son	*fil*
son of	*bar-*
son of	*ben-*
son of	*-ez*

son of	*fitz-*
son of	*mac-, mc-*
son of	*-poulos*
son of	*-s*
son of	*-son, -sen*
son of	*-vich*
song	*cant*
song	*mel*
song	*od*
sooner	*ere*
soothsayer	*augur*
soul	*anima*
soul	*psych*
sound	*ech*
sound	*phon*
sound	*phthong*
sound	*son*
sour	*acid*
sour	*sour*
south	*austral*
south	*meridi*
south	*noto-*
south	*su-*
to sow	*spor*
space	*are*
space	*lacun*
Spanish	*hispan, span*
spark	*scintill*
spasm	*clon*
to speak	*dict*
to speak	*fa, fess*

to speak	*loqu, loc*
to speak	*ora*
to speak	*phe, phas*
to speak	*spek*
spear	*ger*
speech	*lex*
speech	*parl*
speech	*phras*
sphere	*glob*
spider	*arachn*
to spin	*rhomb*
to spin	*spin*
to spin	*turbin*
spine	*acanth*
spine	*rach, rrhach*
spine	*spin*
spiny	*echin*
spiral	*helic*
spirit	*anima*
spirit	*spir*
spirit	*thym*
spittle	*ptyal*
spleen	*lien*
spleen	*splen*
to split	*cleav*
to split	*fiss, -fid*
to split	*schiz, schis*
sponge	*spong*
spoon	*cochl*
spot	*macul*
spread	*patul*

to spread	*strat*
spring	*-burn, -brunn*
to sprout	*blast*
sprout	*clad*
small staff	*bacill*
small staff	*bacter*
stain	*macul*
stalk	*caul*
to stand	*sist*
to stand	*sta, stit*
standing	*stasis, stat*
star	*aster, astr*
star	*sider*
star	*stell*
starch	*amyl*
state	*-acy, -cy*
state	*-age*
state	*-ance*
state	*-ancy*
state	*-asia, -asis*
state	*-asm*
state	*-dom*
state	*-ence*
state	*-ency*
state	*-ery, -ry*
state	*-esis*
state	*-ety*
state	*-hood*
state	*-ion, -tion*
state	*-ism*
state	*-ity*

state	-ment
state	-mony
state	-ness
state (polity)	poli, polit
state	-ship
state	-th
state	-tude
state	-ty
state	-ure
state	-y
to stay	bide
to stay	man
to steal	klept
steam	vap
to steer	ster
stem	stip
stem	stirp
stench	brom
to step	grad, gress
to stick	clam
to stick	cleav
to stick	her, hes
sticky	muc
sticky	visc
stiff	star
to stink	fet
stirrup-bone	staped
to stitch	broc
stock	stirp
stomach	gastr
stomach	ventr

stone	*lapid*
stone	*-lite*
stone	*lith*
stone	*petr*
stone	*sax*
stone	*-stein*
stone	*ston, stan*
straight	*euthy-*
straight	*orth-*
straight	*rect*
straight	*reg*
strange	*xen*
stranger	*barbar*
stranger	*wal*
straw	*carph*
to stretch	*rec*
to stretch	*strec*
to stretch	*tend, tens, tent*
stretched tight	*ten, tenon*
stretching	*ton, ta, tetan*
to strew	*spers*
to strike	*bat*
to strike	*coup*
to strike	*cuss*
to strike	*fend*
to strike	*flict*
to strike	*plaud*
to strike	*plex, pless*
to strike	*sla*
string	*chord*
stroke	*pleg*

strong	*firm*
strong	*fort*
strong	*rob*
strong	*sthen*
to be strong	*val*
Strontian (in Scotland)	*stront*
strontium	*stront*
struggle	*agon*
to struggle	*luct*
study of	*-logy, -ology*
to stuff	*farc*
stumbling-block	*scandal*
stupid	*mor*
stupid	*stult*
stupor	*carotid*
stupor	*narc*
stupor	*stup*
stupor	*torp*
stupor	*typh*
substance	*hyl, yl*
substitute	*vic*
to suffer	*pat, pass*
suffering	*path*
sugar	*sacchar*
sulfur	*sulf, sulph*
sulfur	*thi*
sum	*summ*
to summon	*cit*
sun	*heli*
sun	*sol*
superior	*magister*

to supply	*gar*
to support	*tol*
suture	*raph, raphid, -rrhaph*
to swear	*jur*
to swear	*swer*
sweat	*hidr*
sweat	*sud*
sweet	*dulc*
sweet	*glyc, gluc*
sweet	*suav*
sweet	*swet*
to swell	*bel*
to swell	*blaw*
to swell	*bry*
to swell	*edema*
to swell	*tum*
swelling	*tuber*
to swim	*nect*
to swing	*oscill*
sword	*ens*
sword	*gladi*
sword	*xiph*
system	*-ics*

T

table	*mens*
tail	*caud*
tail	*cerc*
tail	*pen*
tail	*ur*

to take	*cap, cip, cept, ceive*
to take	*empt*
to take	*grip*
to take	*hunt*
to take	*lab, lep*
to take	*prehend, prehens, pris*
to take	*rap*
to take	*sum, sumpt*
tale	*ep*
to talk	*lal*
tanbark	*tann*
Tantalus	*tantal*
to tap (keg)	*broc*
tapeworm	*taen*
taste	*gust*
taste	*sap*
tawny	*fusc*
to teach	*doc*
to teach	*lern*
tear(-drop)	*dacry*
tear(-drop)	*lacrim, lachrym*
tellurium	*tellur*
ten	*dec, deka*
ten	*ten*
ten and	*-teen*
times ten	*-ty*
tender	*pi*
tending toward	*-bund, -bond*
ten thousand	*myria-*
terrible	*din, dein*
to terrify	*gast*

to test	*prob*
testicle	*orchid*
testicle	*test*
thallium	*thall*
thankful	*grat*
thanks	*charis*
that which	*-acle*
that which	*-aire, -air*
that which	*-ant*
that which	*-ate*
that which	*-ent*
that which	*-er*
that which	*-ero*
that which	*-ive*
that which	*-ment*
that which	*-mony*
that which	*-or*
that which	*-th*
that which	*-ty*
that which	*-ure*
the	*al-*
there	*ibi*
thick	*pachy-*
thick	*pycn*
thigh	*femor*
thigh	*mer*
thin	*lept*
thin	*mac*
thin	*tenu*
thing	*re*
thirst	*dips*

thirst	*thirst*
on this side	*cis-, citra-*
Thor	*thor*
thorn	*acanth*
thorn	*spin*
thoroughly	*be-*
thoroughly	*cata-, cath-, cat-*
thoroughly	*com-, co-, col-, con-, cor-*
thoroughly	*en-, em-*
thoroughly	*per-, pel-*
thousand	*kilo-, chilio-*
thousand	*milli-*
thread	*fil*
thread	*mit*
thread	*nemat*
three	*ter*
three	*tri-*
three-dimensional	*stereo-, ster*
threshold	*limin*
throat	*gorg*
throat	*guttur*
throat	*pharyng*
through	*dia-, di-*
through	*per-, pel-*
to throw	*bol, ball*
to throw	*ject, jac*
to throw	*lanc*
to throw	*shot*
to thrust	*trud, trus*
thunder	*bront*
thymus gland	*thym*

thyroid	*thyr*
tibia	*cnem*
to tie	*string, strict*
to till	*col, cult*
time	*chron*
time	*ev*
time	*tempor*
time of	*-ice*
times	*-fold*
times	*-ple*
tin	*stann*
tissue	*hist*
titan	*titan*
to	*ad-*
to	*ob-, oc-, of-, op-*
to be done	*-end, -and*
toe	*digit*
together	*com-, co-, col, con-, cor-*
together	*syn-, syl-, sym-, sys-, sy-*
tomb	*taph*
tone	*ton, ta, tetan*
tongue	*gloss, glot*
tongue	*lingu*
tonsil	*amygdal*
too much	*over-*
tooth	*dent*
tooth	*odont*
top	*apic*
torch	*blaz*
to touch	*hapt, haph, aph, apse*
to touch	*tang, tact*

to touch	*thigma*
toward	*ad-*
toward	*ob-, oc-, of-, op-*
toward	*-ward*
tower	*turr*
town	*-abad*
town	*burg*
town	*-burg, -burgh*
town	*-bury, -borough*
town	*-by*
town	*-dorf, -thorpe*
town	*ham, -heim, home*
town	*-ton*
town	*-ville*
town	*-wich, -wick*
to trade	*merc*
to transport	*perei*
treatment	*therapy*
tree	*dendr*
tribe	*phyl*
trillion	*treg*
trough	*pyel*
true	*etym*
true	*soth*
true	*ver*
trumpet	*salping*
to try	*tempt*
to try out	*per*
tube	*can*
tube	*salping*
tube	*siphon*

tube	*solen*
tube	*syring*
tube	*tub*
to tug	*vuls*
tumor	*-cele*
tumor	*-oma*
tumor	*onc*
Turkey	*turk*
to turn	*rot*
to turn	*stroph, streph, strept*
to turn	*trop*
to turn	*vert, vers*
to turn	*warf*
in turns	*vic*
twelve	*dodeca-*
twelve	*duodec-, duoden-*
twig	*thall*
twin	*didym*
twin	*gemin*
to twist	*tor*
to twist	*wring*
to twist	*writh*
twisted	*plect*
twisted	*strobil*
two	*bi-*
two	*di-*
two	*dicho-*
two	*du-*
two	*dy-*
two	*twi-*
tyrant	*tyrann*

U

uncovered	*gym*
uncovered	*nud*
under	*hypo-, hypn-*
under	*neth*
under	*sub-, suc-, suf-, sug-, sup-, sur-*
under	*under-*
universe	*cosm*
up	*ana-*
upper air	*ether*
upsilon-shaped (U)	*hyo-*
urine	*ur, uret*
urine	*urin*
use	*chres*
to use	*us, ut*
uterus	*hyster*
uterus	*metr*
uterus	*uter*
uvula	*cion*

V

vagina	*colp*
vagina	*vagin*
valley	*dal, tal*
valley	*val*
value	*worth*
Vanadis (goddess)	*vanad*

variation	*para-, par-*
vehicle	*car*
veil	*vel*
vein	*phleb*
(dilated) vein	*varic*
vein	*ven*
velvet	*vill*
vertebra	*spondyl*
vertebra	*vertebr*
vessel	*angi*
vessel	*vas*
view	*-orama*
vinegar	*acet*
violet	*iod, ion*
violet	*porphyr*
violet	*violac*
virgin	*parthen*
virus	*vir*
viscera	*splanchn*
visible	*phaner*
voice	*phthong*
voice	*voc, voke*
to vomit	*emet*
to vow	*vot*
Vulcan	*vulcan*

W

to walk	*ambul*
wall	*mur*

wall	*pariet*
wall	*sept*
to wander	*err*
to wander	*migra*
to wander	*plan*
to wander	*vag*
to want	*desider*
war	*bell*
war	*guerr*
to warn	*moni*
wart	*verruc*
to wash	*lav, lu*
to waste away	*phthis*
wasteland	*heath*
wasting	*tab*
watchman	*gregor*
water	*aqua*
water	*hydat*
water	*hydr*
clear water	*lymph*
wave	*kym, cym*
wave	*und*
wax	*cer*
way	*via*
wealth	*plut*
weapon	*arm*
weapon	*opl*
to wear	*wer*
to weave	*text*
wedge	*cune*

wedge	*sphen*
week	*hebdomad*
to weigh	*grav*
to weigh	*pend, pens*
weight	*bar*
weight	*liber, libr*
weight	*ponder*
well	*bene-*
well	*eu-*
well-born	*gen*
west	*hesper*
west	*occident*
westwind	*zephyr*
wet	*hygr*
whale	*balaen*
whale	*cet*
wheel	*rot*
wheel	*troch*
whip	*flagell*
whirling	*din*
white	*alb*
white	*blanc*
white	*bleach*
white	*cand*
white	*leuc, leuk*
white	*weiss*
whole	*hal*
whole	*hol*
whole	*integr*
wide	*brad*

wide	*eury-*
wide	*lat*
wife	*uxor*
to will	*bul*
to will	*vol*
willow	*salic*
wind	*anem*
wind	*vent*
windbag	*foll*
window	*fenestra*
windpipe	*bronch*
windpipe	*laryng*
windpipe	*trache*
wine	*methy*
wine	*oen, en*
wine	*vin*
wing	*ala*
wing	*pter*
winking	*nictitat*
winter	*hibern*
wisdom	*sap*
wise	*soph*
with	*com-, co-, col-, con-, cor-*
with	*syn-, syl-, sym-, sys-, sy-*
within	*ento-*
within	*eso-*
within	*indi-*
within	*int-*
within	*intro-, intra-*
without	*a-, an-*

without	-less
without	sine
witness	martyr
witness	test
wolf	lup
wolf	lyc
woman	dam
woman	femin
woman	gyn
woman who	-ster
womb	hyster
womb	metr
womb	uter
to wonder	mir
wonder	thaum
wood	hyl, yl
wood	lign
wood	xyl
wool	lan
word	ep
word	lex
word	log
word	parl
word	verb
work	erg, urg
to work	labor
work	oper
to work	wroht
worker	smith
world	mund

worm	*helminth*
worm	*scolec*
worm	*verm*
worship	*-latry*
worthy	*dign*
wound	*traumat*
wound	*vuln*
wreath	*coron*
wretched	*miser*
wrinkle	*rhyt, rut*
wrinkle	*rug*
wrist	*carp*
to write	*graph, gram*
to write	*scrib, script*

Y

year	*ann, enn*
yellow	*flav*
yellow	*chrys*
yellow	*cirr, cirrh*
yellow	*lute*
yellow	*ochr*
yellow	*xanth*
to yield	*cede, ceed, cess*
yoke	*zyg, zeug*
yolk	*lecith*
yolk	*vitell*
young	*hebe*

young	*juven, jun*
Ytterby (in Sweden)	*ytterb*

Z

zinc	*zinc*
zircon	*zircon*

PART TWO

EXERCISES

THE SOURCES OF ENGLISH

English belongs to a very large group of languages which is usually called the Indo-European family, taking its name from that of the earliest known member. Little is known about the Indo-European language or the people who spoke it except that it flourished about 2500 years before Christ and served as the source of most of the western languages in use today and many of the eastern as well.

English belongs to the Germanic branch of the Indo-European family, and specifically to the West Germanic branch from which modern German and Dutch are also descended. Thus a direct line can be traced from the language used by the early Germanic tribes of western Europe to the English language of today. In fact, it is only the words carried by the (Germanic) Anglo-Saxon invaders into Britain that can truly be called native English.

However, borrowing has played fully as large a part as direct inheritance in the shaping of English. The most important sources of borrowed words have been near relatives of the native tongue, other members of the same Indo-European family, notably Old Norse, Latin, French and Greek.

On the next few pages you will see in outline how English, through direct descent and copious borrowing, came to be the language we know today. On the first outline each of the major historical influences is shown, dated approximately, and numbered. The numbers on the outline above are repeated on the chart below where you will find a sample of the part of the English vocabulary affected by each event. The sources shown here have given us very nearly 100% of our language.

A second outline focuses on English alone and gives in greater detail the dates and events which have been important in the history of the language. Again, many of the dates are of necessity only approximate.

Together, these outlines help to explain the very diverse origins of the thousands of English word-roots listed in the dictionary above and presented again in a variety of ways for you to work with in the exercises which follow.

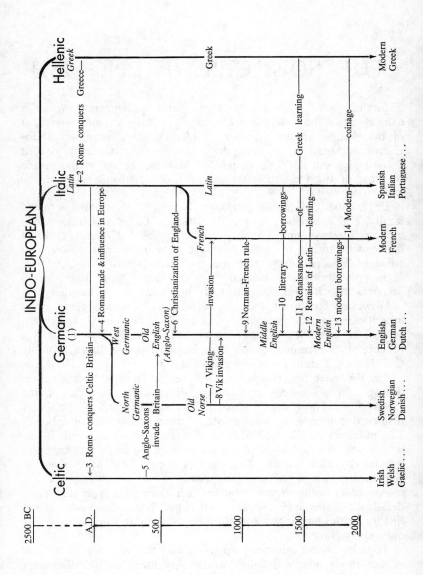

History	Line of Influence	Typical Words Involved
1. Direct descent	Germanic to Modern English	father, wife, child, house, eye, foot, eat, drink, stone, cow, road, lady, girdle
2. Roman conquest of Greece in 2nd C., B.C.	Greek to Latin	philosophy, history, geometry, school, crisis, atomic, meter, music, cynic, bishop, martyr
3. Roman occupation of Britain in 1st–5th C., A.D.	Latin to Celtic	port, (Man-, Win-, Dor-)chester, (War-)wick, (Nor-, Green-)wich
4. Roman military and commercial domination of Europe	Latin to Germanic	kitchen, cup, dish, butter, wine, cheese, pepper, street, mile, inch, Saturday, church
5. Germanic conquest of Celtic Britain after 449	Celtic to Old English (Anglo-Saxon)	York, Thames, London, Avon, Win(-chester), Wor(-cester), Salis(-bury), Cumberland
6. Systematic Christianization of England after 596	Latin to Old English (Anglo-Saxon)	altar, school, box, candle, noon, rule, meter, martyr, verse, priest, beet, radish, pear
7. Norse (Viking) invasion of French coast in 8–9th C.	Old Norse to French	see 8
8. Norse invasion of England in 8–9th C.	Old Norse to Old English	take, get, husband, sister, fellow, happy, law, leg, they, egg, steak, knife, window
9. Norman-French conquest of England in 1066	(Latin to) French to Middle English	nation, property, people, tax, money, city, army, very, nice, music, beef, soup, dinner
10. Direct literary borrowings in translations	Latin to Middle English	popular, quiet, history, nervous, polite, necessary, incredible, subdivide, ulcer
11. Direct, systematic borrowings during Renaissance	Greek to Early Modern English	poem, paragraph, scene, drama, theater, comedy, tragedy, anatomy, thermometer, climax, dialogue
12. Direct, systematic borrowings during Renaissance	Latin to Early Modern English	education, industry, position, item, exist, protest, solid, major, series, maturity
13. Modern borrowings	French to Modern English	machine, parade, garage, corsage, lingerie, divorcee, menu, omelet, casserole, grotesque
14. Modern coinage, largely in technical fields	Latin and Greek to Modern English	scientist, television, automobile, protein, radio, allergy, antibiotic, stereophonic

The Ages of English

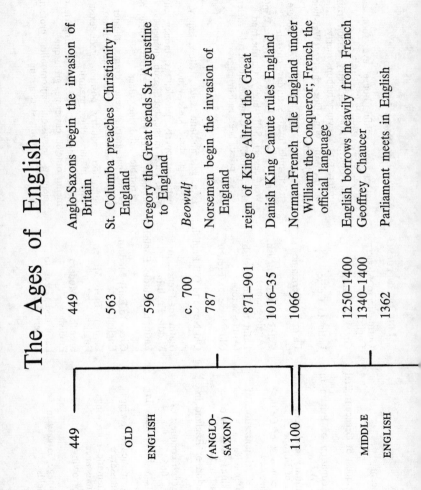

449	449	Anglo-Saxons begin the invasion of Britain
OLD ENGLISH	563	St. Columba preaches Christianity in England
	596	Gregory the Great sends St. Augustine to England
	c. 700	*Beowulf*
(ANGLO-SAXON)	787	Norsemen begin the invasion of England
	871–901	reign of King Alfred the Great
	1016–35	Danish King Canute rules England
1100	1066	Norman-French rule England under William the Conqueror; French the official language
MIDDLE ENGLISH	1250–1400 1340–1400	English borrows heavily from French Geoffrey Chaucer
	1362	Parliament meets in English

1384	Wyclif's translation of the Bible
1475	William Caxton introduces printing into England
15th C.	East Midland (London) dialect becomes dominant
16th C.	peak of the English Renaissance
1564–1616	William Shakespeare
1611	King James Version of the Bible
17th C.	spread of the English language
1755	Samuel Johnson's *Dictionary*
18th C.	growth of American English
1828	Noah Webster's *Dictionary* in America
1928	completion of the *Oxford English Dictionary*
20th C.	vast improvements in transportation, communication and technology; widespread borrowing and coinage of new words

1500

EARLY MODERN ENGLISH

1700

MODERN ENGLISH

Latin Roots

	Root	Meaning
1.	**anima**	*spirit*
2.	**ann, enn**	
3.	**aqua**	
4.	**audi**	
5.	**cad, cid, cas**	
6.	**cap, cip, cept, ceive**	
7.	**capit**	
8.	**-cide, cis**	
9.	**clud, clus, claus, close**	
10.	**cord**	
11.	**corp**	
12.	**cred**	
13.	**dent**	
14.	**dict**	
15.	**duc**	
16.	**fac, fic, fect, -fy**	
17.	**fer**	
18.	**frag, fract**	
19.	**fug**	
20.	**grad, gress**	
21.	**ject, jac**	
22.	**loqu, loc**	
23.	**manu**	
24.	**mater**	
25.	**mit, miss**	

EXAMPLES

animal	animated	inanimate	unanimous

	ROOT	MEANING
26.	**mort**	
27.	**mov, mot, mob**	
28.	**nat, nasc**	
29.	**nomin, nom**	
30.	**pater**	
31.	**pel, puls**	
32.	**pend, pens**	
33.	**plex, plic, ply**	
34.	**pon, pos**	
35.	**reg**	
36.	**scrib, script**	
37.	**sect, sec**	
38.	**sed, sid, sess**	
39.	**sequ, sec**	
40.	**sist**	
41.	**spec, spic**	
42.	**sta, stit**	
43.	**tor**	
44.	**tract**	
45.	**verb**	
46.	**vert, vers**	
47.	**vid, vis**	
48.	**viv**	
49.	**voc, voke**	
50.	**volv, volu**	

EXAMPLES

Greek Roots

	Root	Meaning
1.	**anthrop**	*man, human being*
2.	**aster, astr**	
3.	**bibli**	
4.	**centr**	
5.	**chrom, chro**	
6.	**chron**	
7.	**cosm**	
8.	**-crat, crac**	
9.	**cycl**	
10.	**demo**	
11.	**dyn, dynam**	
12.	**erg, urg**	
13.	**esthet, esthes**	
14.	**gam**	
15.	**ge**	
16.	**gnos, gnom**	
17.	**gon**	
18.	**graph, gram**	
19.	**gyn**	
20.	**heli**	
21.	**hydr**	
22.	**iatr**	
23.	**kine-, cinema-**	
24.	**lith**	
25.	**log**	

EXAMPLES

anthropology   anthropoid   misanthrope

_____

_____

_____

_____

_____

_____

_____

_____

_____

_____

_____

_____

_____

_____

_____

_____

_____

_____

_____

_____

_____

_____

_____

	ROOT	MEANING
26.	-logy	
27.	mania	
28.	meter, metr	
29.	morph	
30.	nom	
31.	odont	
32.	onym, onoma	
33.	op	
34.	phan, phen	
35.	phil	
36.	phob	
37.	phon	
38.	phot, phos	
39.	pod, pus	
40.	poli, polit	
41.	scop	
42.	som, somat	
43.	soph	
44.	tax, tact	
45.	techn	
46.	the, theo	
47.	therm	
48.	thes, thet	
49.	top	
50.	trop	

EXAMPLES

Anglo-Saxon (Old English) Roots

	ROOT	MEANING
1.	**ber**	*to carry, to bear*
2.	**bid, bead**	
3.	**bind**	
4.	**blaw**	
5.	**bleach**	
6.	**brek**	
7.	**brew**	
8.	**burn, bran**	
9.	**dear**	
10.	**drag**	
11.	**drif**	
12.	**drink**	
13.	**dryg**	
14.	**fare**	
15.	**fed**	
16.	**flot**	
17.	**fot, fet**	
18.	**hard, -ard**	
19.	**hel**	
20.	**hev**	
21.	**lack**	
22.	**laf**	
23.	**leap**	
24.	**led**	
25.	**lern**	

Examples

bear berth born borne burden bore

	Root	Meaning
26.	lik	
27.	los	
28.	mark	
29.	reck	
30.	rob, rev	
31.	say	
32.	shuf	
33.	side	
34.	sit, set	
35.	sla	
36.	spell	
37.	spin	
38.	stall	
39.	star	
40.	ster	
41.	swer	
42.	tell, tal	
43.	tes	
44.	tru	
45.	wak	
46.	ward	
47.	wit, wis	
48.	wring	
49.	writh	
50.	wroht	

EXAMPLES

Prefixes

LATIN:

	PREFIX	MEANING
1.	ab-	*away, from*
2.	ad-	
3.	ante-	
4.	circum-	
5.	com-	
6.	contra-, counter-	
7.	de-	
8.	dis-	
9.	e-, ex-	
10.	inter-	
11.	intro-, intra-	
12.	ob-	
13.	per-, pel-	
14.	post-	
15.	pre-, prae-	
16.	pro-	
17.	re-	
18.	se-	
19.	sub-	
20.	super-	
21.	trans-, tra-	

EXAMPLES

absent   abrupt   aberration   abject

_____

_____

_____

_____

_____

_____

_____

_____

_____

_____

_____

_____

_____

_____

_____

_____

_____

GREEK:

Prefix	Meaning
22. **a-, an-**	
23. **anti-, ant-**	
24. **apo-, ap-**	
25. **cata-**	
26. **dia-, di-**	
27. **ec-**	
28. **epi-, ep-**	
29. **eu-**	
30. **hetero-**	
31. **homo-**	
32. **hyper-**	
33. **hypo-, hyp-**	
34. **meta-, met-**	
35. **micro-**	
36. **orth-**	
37. **para-, par-**	
38. **peri-**	
39. **syn-**	
40. **tele-**	

EXAMPLES

ANGLO-SAXON:

	Prefix	Meaning
41.	a-	
42.	be-	
43.	for-	
44.	fore-	
45.	n-	
46.	out-	
47.	over-	
48.	un-	
49.	under-	
50.	with-	

EXAMPLES

Latin Prefixes

Write a root-definition for each of the following words:

FER: *to carry, to bear*

interfere	*between—to carry*
transfer	
circumference	
infer	
suffer	
offer	
afferent	
efferent	
defer	
refer	
confer	
prefer	
proffer	

MIT, MISS: *to send*

intermittent	
intermission	
transmit	
transmission	
submit	
submission	
admit	
emit	

demise   _____

remit   _____

committee   _____

premise   _____

promise   _____

In each space write the words formed from the prefix-root combinations.

	DUC *to lead*	FER *to bear*	JECT *to throw*	SCRIB SCRIPT *to write*	PON POS *to put*
PRO- *forward*					
DE- *down* *away*					
RE- *back* *again*			*reject* *rejected* *rejection*		
IN-, IM- *in* *into*					
CON-, COM- *together* *with*					

Number Roots

Meaning	Root(s)
half	*hemi, demi, semi, med*
one	
two	
three	
four	
five	
six	
seven	
eight	
nine	
ten	
plus ten	
times ten	
hundred	
thousand	
ten thousand	
million	
first	
both	
equal	
few	
many	
all	

EXAMPLES

hemisphere   demitasse   semi-colon   medium

Suffixes

Suffix	Meaning
1. -able	*able to (be)*
2. -ac, -iac	
3. -acious	
4. -acy, -cy	
5. -age	
6. -al	
7. -ance	
8. -ancy	
9. -ary, -arium	
10. -dom	
11. -ee	
12. -eer	
13. -en (v.)	
14. -ence	
15. -ency	
16. -er, -yer	
17. -ery	
18. -escent	
19. -esis	
20. -eur	
21. -ferous	
22. -fold	
23. -ful	
24. -fy	
25. -hood	

EXAMPLES

adaptable   reliable   avoidable

_____

_____

_____

_____

_____

_____

_____

_____

_____

_____

_____

_____

_____

_____

_____

_____

_____

_____

_____

_____

_____

_____

	SUFFIX	MEANING
26.	-ic	
27.	-ical	
28.	-ier	
29.	-ine	
30.	-ion, -tion	
31.	-ish	
32.	-ism	
33.	-ist	
34.	-ium	
35.	-ive (adj.)	
36.	-ize, -ise	
37.	-less	
38.	-ly (adj.)	
39.	-ly (adv.)	
40.	-ness	
41.	-oid, -oda, -ode	
42.	-or	
43.	-ory, -orium	
44.	-ose	
45.	-ous	
46.	-ship	
47.	-some	
48.	-ulent	
49.	-ward	
50.	-wise	

Examples

Diminutives

Some diminutive suffixes:

-cle	-et	-kin	-ock	-y
-cule	-ette	-let	-ula	
-el	-ie	-ling	-ule	

Fill each of the blanks below with a word which uses a diminutive suffix.

1. little book — B _ o o k l e _ T
2. little James — J _____ Y
3. little part — P _____ E
4. little sphere — S _____ E
5. little cigar — C _____ T
6. little verse — V _____ E
7. little relative — S _____ G
8. little Paul — P _____ E
9. little skin — C _____ E
10. little prince — P _____ G
11. little key — C _____ E
12. little tablecloth — N _____ N
13. little pig — P _____ T
14. little body — C _____ E
15. little pearl — M _____ E
16. little man — M _____ N
17. little closed place — C _____ T
18. little bull — B _____ K
19. little heap — M _____ E
20. little precious one — D _____ G
21. little joint — A _____ E
22. little mouse — M _____ E

23.	little goose	G	_____	G
24.	little song	C	_____	E
25.	little hill	H	_____	K
26.	little box	C	_____	E
27.	son of little Will	W	_____	N
28.	little animal of one year	Y	_____	G
29.	little root	R	_____	E
30.	little lame one	C	_____	E
31.	little brain	C	_____	M
32.	little form	F	_____	A
33.	little finger-length fish	F	_____	G
34.	little something new	N	_____	L
35.	little stomach	G	_____	A
36.	little tree from a seed	S	_____	G
37.	little tree	S	_____	G
38.	little cell	C	_____	E
39.	little bud	B	_____	A
40.	little statue	S	_____	E
41.	little feathered one	F	_____	G
42.	little knot	N	_____	E
43.	little abandoned infant	F	_____	G
44.	little animal	A	_____	E
45.	little duck	D	_____	G
46.	little hanging thing	P	_____	M
47.	little (St.) Peter	P	_____	L
48.	little cat	K	_____	Y
49.	little-body device	C	_____	T
50.	son of little Tom	T	_____	N

Medical Roots

Root	Meaning
1. **aden**	*gland*
2. **alg**	
3. **angi**	
4. **anter-**	
5. **arthr, art**	
6. **brady-**	
7. **bronch**	
8. **burs**	
9. **card**	
10. **cephal**	
11. **chir, cheir**	
12. **chol**	
13. **chondr**	
14. **cocc**	
15. **crani**	
16. **cyst**	
17. **derm**	
18. **ecto-**	
19. **endo-**	
20. **enter**	
21. **gangli**	
22. **gastr**	
23. **hem, haem, em**	
24. **hepat**	
25. **hyster**	

EXAMPLES

adenoids adenalgia myxadenitis

	ROOT	MEANING
26.	-ia	
27.	-itis	
28.	mast	
29.	my	
30.	myel	
31.	nephr	
32.	neur	
33.	-oma	
34.	ophthalm	
35.	-osis, -sis	
36.	oste	
37.	ot	
38.	path	
39.	phleb	
40.	pneumon, pneum, pne	
41.	poster-	
42.	proct	
43.	psych	
44.	ren	
45.	rhin	
46.	-rrhea	
47.	stom	
48.	tach	
49.	tom, tme	
50.	trache	

Examples

Biological Roots

	ROOT	MEANING
1.	**amoeb**	*change, amoeba*
2.	**annel, annul**	
3.	**anth**	
4.	**auto-**	
5.	**bio**	
6.	**blast**	
7.	**bucc**	
8.	**capill**	
9.	**cav**	
10.	**cervic**	
11.	**chias**	
12.	**chord**	
13.	**chyl**	
14.	**chym**	
15.	**cili**	
16.	**clas**	
17.	**coel, cel**	
18.	**cyt**	
19.	**dur**	
20.	**eco-, oec**	
21.	**ento-**	
22.	**foramin**	
23.	**gen**	
24.	**gym**	
25.	**hist**	

EXAMPLES

amoebic   amoebiform   amoebotaenia

	ROOT	MEANING
26.	lamin, lamell	
27.	lemm	
28.	macro-	
29.	meso-	
30.	nemat	
31.	ov	
32.	palp	
33.	phag	
34.	phyt	
35.	plas	
36.	pulm, pulmon	
37.	ram	
38.	sarc	
39.	scler	
40.	sinus, sinu	
41.	squam	
42.	thec	
43.	trich, thrix	
44.	vag	
45.	vagin	
46.	vesic	
47.	vita	
48.	vitell	
49.	zo	
50.	zyg, zeug	

EXAMPLES

Animals in Words

	WORD	MEANING AND REASON
1.	**porcupine**	spiny pig—from appearance
2.	**canary**	
3.	**easel**	
4.	**dandelion**	
5.	**impecunious**	
6.	**halibut**	
7.	**Capri**	
8.	**cancer**	
9.	**chameleon**	
10.	**muscle**	
11.	**alligator**	
12.	**fellow**	
13.	**Alcatraz**	
14.	**bugle**	
15.	**Beverley**	
16.	**pedigree**	
17.	**chevron**	
18.	**polecat**	
19.	**formic acid**	
20.	**Turin**	
21.	**cab**	
22.	**cynosure**	
23.	**marshal**	
24.	**Arctic**	
25.	**cynic**	

	WORD	MEANING AND REASON
26.	**chivalry**	
27.	**porcelain**	
28.	**hippopotamus**	
29.	**presbytery**	
30.	**peculiar**	
31.	**bellwether**	
32.	**Bernard**	
33.	**buffalo**	
34.	**porpoise**	
35.	**kennel**	
36.	**priest**	
37.	**aviator**	
38.	**cavalcade**	

Animal Adjectives

	WORD	ROOT	ANIMAL
39.	**canine**	*can*	dog
40.	**porcine**		
41.	**leonine**		
42.	**lupine**		
43.	**asinine**		
44.	**feline**		
45.	**bovine**		
46.	**aquiline**		
47.	**serpentine**		
48.	**piscine**		
49.	**vulpine**		
50.	**equine**		

Colors in Words

	WORD	ROOT	COLOR
1.	chlorine	*chlor*	green
2.	melancholy		
3.	Argentina		
4.	iodine		
5.	chrysanthemum		
6.	rubric		
7.	albino		
8.	denigrate		
9.	leucocyte		
10.	chlorophyll		
11.	praseodymium		
12.	cirrhosis		
13.	fulvous		
14.	Ethiopia		
15.	iris		
16.	panchromatic		
17.	aureole		
18.	atrocious		
19.	bleachers		
20.	viridescent		
21.	Chrysostom		
22.	rhododendron		
23.	Maurice		
24.	albumen		
25.	rubella		

	Word	Root	Color
26.	cyanosis		
27.	polio		
28.	argentiferous		
29.	Colorado		
30.	ruby		
31.	phoenix		
32.	flavid		
33.	caesium		
34.	chrysalis		
35.	Melanesia		
36.	platinum		
37.	leukemia		
38.	glaucoma		
39.	oriole		
40.	chromosome		
41.	Rhode Island		
42.	xanthoderma		
43.	cyanide		
44.	riboflavin		
45.	candidate		
46.	Blanche		
47.	appalling		
48.	edelweiss		
49.	Rufus		
50.	album		

People in Words

	WORD	NAME
1.	**saxophone**	*Antoine J. (Adolphe) Sax*
2.	**maudlin**	
3.	**sadist**	
4.	**tawdry**	
5.	**pander**	
6.	**philippic**	
7.	**chauvinism**	
8.	**epicurean**	
9.	**quixotic**	
10.	**amazon**	
11.	**boycott**	
12.	**macadam**	
13.	**czar**	
14.	**solon**	
15.	**pants**	
16.	**martial**	
17.	**silhouette**	
18.	**derrick**	
19.	**volt**	
20.	**nicotine**	
21.	**dunce**	
22.	**crisscross**	
23.	**atlas**	
24.	**ammonia**	
25.	**camellia**	

Reason

invented the instrument

	WORD	NAME
26.	**panic**	
27.	**guillotine**	
28.	**lynch**	
29.	**mentor**	
30.	**cereal**	
31.	**America**	
32.	**tantalize**	
33.	**volcano**	
34.	**derby**	
35.	**guppy**	
36.	**sandwich**	
37.	**venereal**	
38.	**aphrodisiac**	
39.	**martinet**	
40.	**pasteurize**	
41.	**titanic**	
42.	**cardigan**	
43.	**morphine**	
44.	**masochist**	
45.	**maverick**	
46.	**groggy**	
47.	**brag**	
48.	**Bolivia**	
49.	**guy**	
50.	**mausoleum**	

REASON

Places in Words

	WORD	PLACE
1.	millinery	*Milan, Italy*
2.	bedlam	
3.	stoic	
4.	stygian	
5.	meander	
6.	labyrinth	
7.	pandemonium	
8.	maelstrom	
9.	laconic	
10.	olympian	
11.	academy	
12.	bourbon	
13.	cologne	
14.	frankfurter	
15.	artesian	
16.	cravat	
17.	wiener	
18.	denim	
19.	hamburger	
20.	peach	
21.	attic	
22.	tangerine	
23.	bayonet	
24.	currant	
25.	cantaloupe	

REASON

center for women's finery in 16th Century

	WORD	PLACE
26.	**solecism**	
27.	**copper**	
28.	**cashmere**	
29.	**calico**	
30.	**tuxedo**	
31.	**turquoise**	
32.	**sherry**	
33.	**port (wine)**	
34.	**gypsy**	
35.	**worsted**	
36.	**canary**	
37.	**limousine**	
38.	**damask**	
39.	**walnut**	
40.	**dollar**	
41.	**arras**	
42.	**vaudeville**	
43.	**bungalow**	
44.	**roquefort**	
45.	**canter**	
46.	**burgundy**	
47.	**indigo**	
48.	**magnet**	
49.	**sybaritic**	
50.	**spaniel**	

REASON

_____
_____
_____
_____
_____
_____
_____
_____
_____
_____
_____
_____
_____
_____
_____
_____
_____
_____
_____
_____
_____
_____
_____
_____
_____

Words from Latin—I

	WORD	ROOT-DEFINITION
1.	**contradict**	*against—to speak*
2.	**inspector**	
3.	**president**	
4.	**centigrade**	
5.	**refuge**	
6.	**dentifrice**	
7.	**loquacious**	
8.	**incredible**	
9.	**prelude**	
10.	**annihilate**	
11.	**magnify**	
12.	**progress**	
13.	**incisor**	
14.	**translate**	
15.	**decadent**	
16.	**independent**	
17.	**distort**	
18.	**omnivorous**	
19.	**contemporary**	
20.	**exit**	
21.	**innate**	
22.	**unison**	
23.	**aquamarine**	
24.	**decapitate**	
25.	**concourse**	

OTHER EXAMPLES

contrary   contrast   predict   dictionary

_____

_____

_____

_____

_____

_____

_____

_____

_____

_____

_____

_____

_____

_____

_____

_____

_____

_____

_____

_____

_____

	WORD	ROOT-DEFINITION
26.	**subscribe**	
27.	**intersection**	
28.	**confide**	
29.	**revolution**	
30.	**anniversary**	
31.	**infinite**	
32.	**repulsive**	
33.	**immortal**	
34.	**attract**	
35.	**resist**	
36.	**nominate**	
37.	**conspiracy**	
38.	**corpulent**	
39.	**vivacious**	
40.	**concord**	
41.	**audition**	
42.	**verbose**	
43.	**paternity**	
44.	**interference**	
45.	**complex**	
46.	**proponent**	
47.	**consequent**	
48.	**missile**	
49.	**somnambulist**	
50.	**exclusive**	

OTHER EXAMPLES

_____

_____

_____

_____

_____

_____

_____

_____

_____

_____

_____

_____

_____

_____

_____

_____

_____

_____

_____

_____

_____

_____

_____

_____

_____

Words from Latin—II

	ROOT-DEFINITION	WORD
1.	out—to push	*expel*
2.	after—to place	
3.	gnaw—ing	
4.	away—to scrape	
5.	against—to build	
6.	clear—to make	
7.	back—into—bag	
8.	not—injure—ing	
9.	drag—that which	
10.	three—teeth	
11.	sacred—to make	
12.	down—to laugh	
13.	before—run—one who	
14.	back—to bend	
15.	not—strong—place where	
16.	middle—age—related to	
17.	out—root—to do	
18.	together—seek—one who	
19.	rule—ing	
20.	all—know—ing	
21.	not—please—able	
22.	back—to bite	
23.	apart—flock—to make	
24.	twist—having the quality of	
25.	pledge—one who	

Other Examples

extricate   exodus   repellent   propeller

	ROOT-DEFINITION	WORD
26.	away—to advise	
27.	touch—ing	
28.	together—stars—state	
29.	to hold—having quality of	
30.	not—fit	
31.	one—shape	
32.	road—to lead	
33.	voice—bearing	
34.	together—run—ing	
35.	not—conquer—able	
36.	thoroughly—strong—becoming	
37.	forward—to thrust	
38.	in—to flow—act	
39.	witness—to make	
40.	through—breathe	
41.	sun—place where	
42.	without—care	
43.	not—out—to pray—able	
44.	rise—ing	
45.	many—side—related to	
46.	away—wash—act	
47.	bear—able—to make	
48.	not—together—stick—ing	
49.	out of—ground	
50.	toward—heavy—to make	

OTHER EXAMPLES

Words from Greek–I

	WORD	ROOT-DEFINITION
1.	**atom**	*not—cut*
2.	**cosmopolitan**	
3.	**pentagon**	
4.	**pantomime**	
5.	**schizophrenia**	
6.	**philanthropist**	
7.	**anonymous**	
8.	**telegram**	
9.	**tripod**	
10.	**chromosome**	
11.	**autonomy**	
12.	**odometer**	
13.	**monolithic**	
14.	**acrophobia**	
15.	**eucalyptus**	
16.	**megaphone**	
17.	**encephalitis**	
18.	**taxidermist**	
19.	**cardiac**	
20.	**amphibious**	
21.	**Cyclops**	
22.	**psychosomatic**	
23.	**photograph**	
24.	**atheist**	
25.	**sympathy**	

OTHER EXAMPLES

atypical   amoral   dichotomy   anatomy

	Word	Root-Definition
26.	**chiropractor**	
27.	**technical**	
28.	**anemia**	
29.	**misanthropic**	
30.	**euthanasia**	
31.	**hippopotamus**	
32.	**pediatrician**	
33.	**bibliophile**	
34.	**microscope**	
35.	**autobiography**	
36.	**astronomy**	
37.	**geriatrics**	
38.	**diagnosis**	
39.	**amorphous**	
40.	**bigamist**	
41.	**geophysical**	
42.	**isotherm**	
43.	**neuritis**	
44.	**democrat**	
45.	**antipyretic**	
46.	**epitaph**	
47.	**geography**	
48.	**misogynist**	
49.	**orthodontia**	
50.	**trigonometry**	

OTHER EXAMPLES

Words from Greek—II

	ROOT-DEFINITION	WORD
1.	solid—sound—related to	*stereophonic*
2.	copy—to write	
3.	heat—to measure	
4.	against—struggle—one who	
5.	down—to turn	
6.	black—bile—state	
7.	three—circle	
8.	home—order—related to	
9.	good—word—act	
10.	through—to flow	
11.	many—marriage—state	
12.	terrible—lizard	
13.	small—universe	
14.	mind—heal—one who	
15.	first—model	
16.	without—feeling—condition	
17.	time—measure	
18.	whole—to burn	
19.	man—study of	
20.	one—to rule	
21.	badly—nourished—state	
22.	joint—inflammation	
23.	up—cut—state	
24.	white—blood—condition	
25.	sun—element	

OTHER EXAMPLES

stereotype   cholesterol   phonetic   phonograph

_____

_____

_____

_____

_____

_____

_____

_____

_____

_____

_____

_____

_____

_____

_____

_____

_____

_____

_____

_____

_____

_____

_____

_____

Root-Definition	Word
26. around—measure	
27. birth—act	
28. together—name	
29. under—skin	
30. love—wisdom—one who	
31. small—to look	
32. sign—to carry	
33. not—remember—condition	
34. all—view	
35. straight—child—one who	
36. green—leaf	
37. without—feeling—state	
38. colored—body	
39. hidden—to write	
40. to digest—related to	
41. without—rule—state	
42. to love—tree	
43. good—death—condition	
44. blood—to flow	
45. light—measure	
46. beyond—to carry	
47. new—plant	
48. together—arrangement	
49. around—to look	
50. wise—stupid	

OTHER EXAMPLES

Words from One Root

GEN: *cause, birth, kind, race*

1. to cause
   G E N e r a t e

2. a cause of electricity
   G E N _ _ _ _ _ r

3. to cause anew
   _ _ G E N _ _ a _ _

4. a chemical cause of water
   _ y _ _ _ G E N

5. a chemical cause of niter
   _ _ _ _ o G E N

6. (a condition) caused by the mind (adj.)
   p _ _ _ _ _ G E N _ _

7. causing a good photograph
   _ _ _ _ _ G E N _ c

8. birth
   G E N _ _ i _

9. tending to give birth
   G E N _ _ _ _ _ v _

10. to beget
    _ _ G E N d _ _

11. one who begets
    p _ _ G E N _ _ _ _

12. one set of births
    G E N _ _ _ _ i _ _

13. relating to heredity

    G E N _ t _ _

14. the study of heredity

    G E N _ _ _ _ s

15. that which transmits hereditary traits

    G E N _

16. a study of births (family tree)

    G E N _ a _ _ _ _

17. offspring

    _ r _ G E N _

18. mating superior human beings

    e _ G E N _ _ _

19. pertaining to reproduction

    G E N _ _ _ l

20. the organs of reproduction

    G E N _ t _ _ _

21. existing from birth

    _ o _ G E N _ _ _ _

22. the origin of man

    a _ _ _ _ _ _ _ G E N _ _ _ _

23. native born (not imported)

    _ _ d _ G E N _ _ _

24. leaving the estate to the first-born male

    _ _ _ _ _ G E N _ _ u _ _

25. well-born (proper name)

    _ _ G E N e

26. refined (well-born)
    G E N _ _ _ e _

27. refinement
    G E N _ _ _ _ _ _ y

28. one who is born brilliant
    G E N i _ _

29. having inborn talent; clever
    i _ G E N _ _ _ _

30. of good (family) stock; magnanimous
    G E N _ r _ _ _ _

31. the well-born class (now usually humorous)
    G E N t _ _

32. gifted at birth; happy
    G E N _ a _

33. of a kind to be happy with others
    _ o _ G E N _ _ _

34. a man who is "well-born" and refined
    G E N _ _ _ m _ _

35. freeborn, frank, simple, gullible
    _ _ G E N u _ _ _

36. a simple, naive girl
    i _ G E N _ _

37. to fall away from the (good) kind
    _ _ G E N _ _ _ _ e

38. a major class or kind
    G E N u _

39. a sexual class or kind
    G E N _ _ r

40. an artistic class or kind
    G E N r _

41. pertaining to a class or kind
    G E N _ _ i _

42. pertaining to all of a class or kind
    G E N _ _ _ l

43. of the true kind; authentic
    G E N _ i _ _

44. of the same kind throughout
    h _ _ _ G E N _ _ _ _

45. made to be of the same kind throughout
    _ _ _ _ G E N _ z _ _

46. composed of different kinds
    _ _ t _ _ _ G E N _ _ _ _

47. a group of individuals of the same kind (biol.)
    GE N _ _ _ p _

48. a member of the non-Jewish race
    G E N _ _ _ e

49. mixture of races
    m _ _ _ _ G E N _ _ _ _ _

50. killing of a race
    G E N _ _ _ d _

Word-Pairs

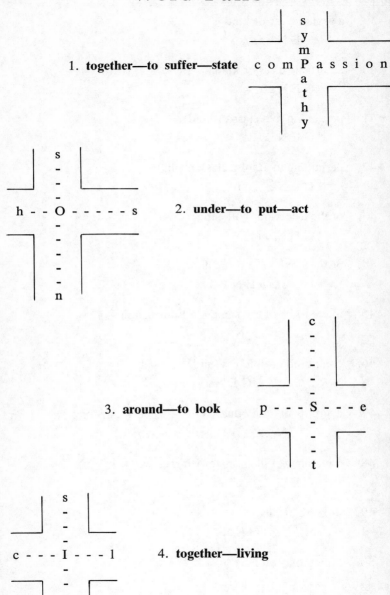

1. **together—to suffer—state**

```
              s
              y
              m
c o m P a s s i o n
              a
              t
              h
              y
```

2. **under—to put—act**

```
      s
      -
      -
      -
h - - O - - - - - s
      -
      -
      -
      -
      n
```

3. **around—to look**

```
          c
          -
          -
          -
p - - - S - - - e
          -
          -
          t
```

4. **together—living**

```
      s
      -
      -
c - - I - - - l
      -
      -
      c
```

5. **together—time**

6. **around—to carry**

7. **right-angled**

8. **many-fold**

9. **love—having the quality of**

```
 _|  -  |_
    -
- - O - - c
    -
 _|  -  |_
    -
    s
```

```
 _|  -  |_
    -
    -
    -
- - R - - - r
    -
    -
    -
    r  |
```

10. **over—to see—one who**

11. **below—skin—related to**

```
         -
         -
         -
- - - - - - - - E - - S
         -
         -
         c
```

12. **many-tongued**

```
 _|  -  |
    -
    -
    -
    -
- - L - - - - t
    -
    -
    -
    -
    l  |
```

13. **bear—related to**

```
            u
            -
- - - - I   c
            -
            -
```

```
    -
    -
c - N - - - - - -
    -
    -
    -
    e
```

14. **together—to run**

15. **through—to turn—act**

```
            p
            -
            -
            -
- - - - - R - - - - - m
            -
            -
            -
```

```
    -
    -
    -
e - - O - -
    -
    -
    -
    -
    -
    e
```

16. **into—body**

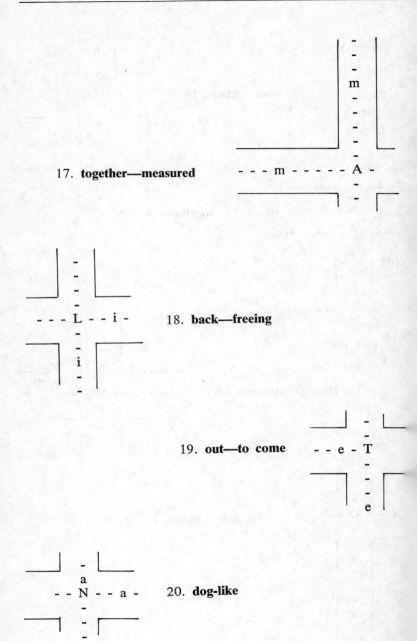

17. **together—measured**

18. **back—freeing**

19. **out—to come**

20. **dog-like**

Word-Chain

Find the missing links.

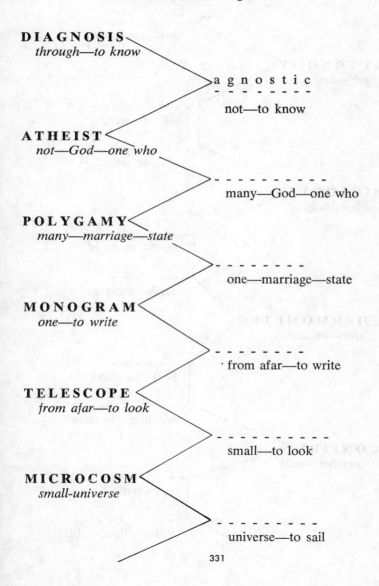

DIAGNOSIS
through—to know

a g n o s t i c
- - - - - - - -
not—to know

ATHEIST
not—God—one who

- - - - - - - - - -
many—God—one who

POLYGAMY
many—marriage—state

- - - - - - - - -
one—marriage—state

MONOGRAM
one—to write

· from afar—to write

TELESCOPE
from afar—to look

- - - - - - - - -
small—to look

MICROCOSM
small-universe

- - - - - - - -
universe—to sail

331

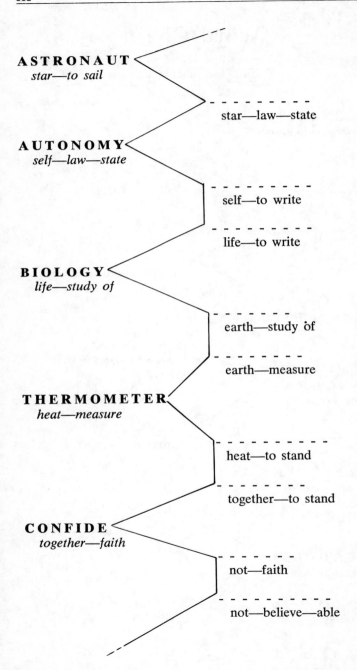

ASTRONAUT
star—to sail

star—law—state

AUTONOMY
self—law—state

self—to write

life—to write

BIOLOGY
life—study of

earth—study of

earth—measure

THERMOMETER
heat—measure

heat—to stand

together—to stand

CONFIDE
together—faith

not—faith

not—believe—able

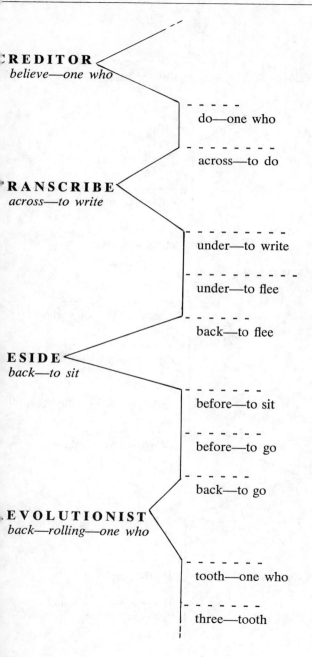

CREDITOR
believe—one who

do—one who

across—to do

TRANSCRIBE
across—to write

under—to write

under—to flee

back—to flee

BESIDE
back—to sit

before—to sit

before—to go

back—to go

EVOLUTIONIST
back—rolling—one who

tooth—one who

three—tooth

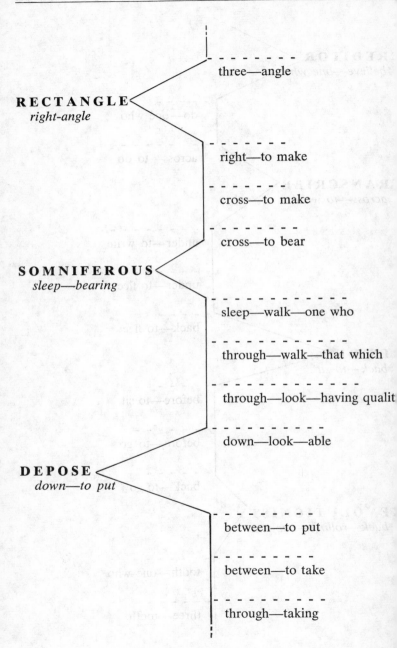

RECTANGLE
right-angle

three—angle

right—to make

cross—to make

cross—to bear

SOMNIFEROUS
sleep—bearing

sleep—walk—one who

through—walk—that which

through—look—having qualit

down—look—able

DEPOSE
down—to put

between—to put

between—to take

through—taking

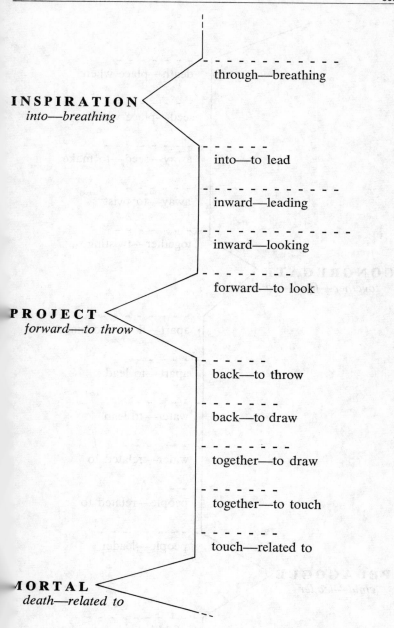

INSPIRATION
into—breathing

through—breathing

into—to lead

inward—leading

inward—looking

forward—to look

PROJECT
forward—to throw

back—to throw

back—to draw

together—to draw

together—to touch

touch—related to

MORTAL
death—related to

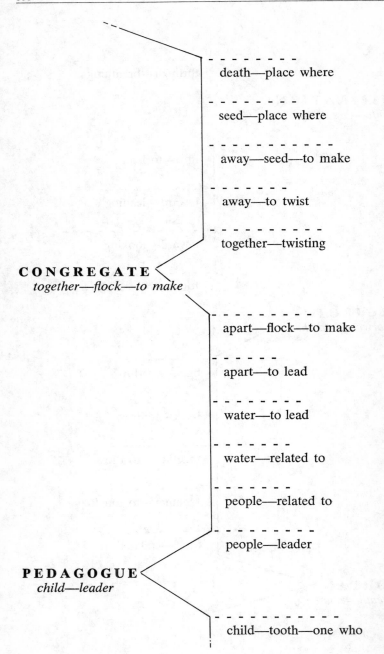

death—place where

seed—place where

away—seed—to make

away—to twist

together—twisting

CONGREGATE
together—flock—to make

apart—flock—to make

apart—to lead

water—to lead

water—related to

people—related to

people—leader

PEDAGOGUE
child—leader

child—tooth—one who

straight—tooth—one who

straight—write—act

shake—write—act

shake—measure

head—measure—act

ENCEPHALITIS
in—head—inflammation

nose—inflammation

nose—to look

ear—to look

ear—study of

fungus—study of

earth—fungus

middle—earth—related to

INTERMEDIARY
between—middle—one who

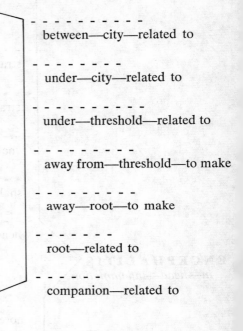

between—city—related to

under—city—related to

under—threshold—related to

away from—threshold—to make

away—root—to make

root—related to

companion—related to

SOCIETY
companion—state

Bibliography

STANDARD AND ETYMOLOGICAL DICTIONARIES

The American College Dictionary. New York: Random House, 1962. 1444 pp.

Collocott, T. C. (ed.), *Chambers' English Dictionary.* Totowa, N.J.: Littlefield, Adams & Co. (SOS 166), 1965. 380 pp., paper.

Gove, Philip B. (ed.), *Webster's Third New International Dictionary.* Springfield, Mass.: 1963. 2662 pp.

MacDonald, A. M. (ed.), *Chambers' Etymological English Dictionary.* Totowa, N.J.: Littlefield, Adams & Co. (SOS 153), 1964. 784 pp., paper.

Matthews, Mitford, *Dictionary of Americanisms,* one volume edition. Chicago: University of Chicago Press, 1951. 1946 pp.

Murray, James A. H. (ed.), *Oxford English Dictionary.* 13 vols. Oxford: Clarendon Press, 1961.

Onions, C. T. (ed.), *The Oxford Universal Dictionary.* Oxford: Clarendon Press, 1955. 2515 pp.

Partridge, Eric, *Origins, a Short Etymological Dictionary of Modern English.* New York: The Macmillan Company, 1961. 972 pp.

Shipley, Joseph T., *Dictionary of Word Origins.* Totowa, N.J.: Littlefield, Adams & Co. (SOS 121), 1964. 430 pp., paper.

Skeat, Walter W., *A Concise Etymological Dictionary of the English Language.* New York: Capricorn Books (Cap Giant 235), 1963. 656 pp.

Standard College Dictionary. New York: Harcourt, Brace & World, 1963. 1606 pp.

Webster's New World Dictionary of the American Language. New York: The World Publishing Company, 1951. 1724 pp.

Webster's Seventh New Collegiate Dictionary. Springfield, Mass.: G. & C. Merriam Co., 1963. 1220 pp.

MEDICAL AND BIOLOGICAL TERMINOLOGY

Abercrombie, M., C. J. Hickman and M. L. Johnson, *A Dictionary of Biology.* Baltimore: Penguin Books (R 3), 1951. 254 pp., paper.

Agard, Walter R., and Herbert M. Howe, *Medical Greek and Latin at a Glance.* New York: Harper & Brothers (Hoeber-Harper Books), 1960. 96 pp.

Dorland's Illustrated Medical Dictionary. Philadelphia: W. B. Saunders Co., 1957. 1598 pp.

Jaeger, Edmund C., *A Source-Book of Biological Names and Terms,* 3rd edition. Springfield, Ill.: Charles C. Thomas, 1955. 323 pp.

Medical Etymology, teaching copy, reprinted from *Stedman's Medical Dictionary,* 20th edition. Baltimore: The Williams & Wilkins Co., 1961. 31 pp., paper.

Pepper, O. H. Perry, *Medical Etymology.* Philadelphia: W. B. Saunders Co., 1959. 263 pp.

Schifferes, Justus J., *Schifferes' Family Medical Encyclopedia.* New York: Permabooks (M 5013), 1959. 619 pp., paper.

Skinner, Henry Alan, *The Origin of Medical Terms,* 2nd edition. Baltimore: The Williams & Wilkins Co., 1961. 438 pp.

Stedman's Medical Dictionary, 20th edition. Baltimore: The Williams & Wilkins Co., 1961. 1680 pp.

Swartz, Harry, *Layman's Medical Dictionary.* New York: Frederick Ungar Publishing Co., 1955. 306 pp., paper.

Yancy, Patrick H., S. J., *Origins from Mythology of Biological Names and Terms,* 2nd edition. Mobile, Ala.: Spring Hill College Press, 1961. 47 pp., paper.

SCIENTIFIC TERMINOLOGY

English, Horace B., and Ava C. English, *A Comprehensive Dictionary of Psychological and Phychoanalytical Terms.* New York: Longmans, Green & Co., 1959. 595 pp.

Flood, W. E., *Dictionary of Chemical Names.* Totowa, N.J.: Littlefield, Adams & Co. (SOS 147), 1963. 238 pp., paper.

Gaynor, Frank, *Concise Dictionary of Science.* Totowa, N.J.: Littlefield, Adams & Co. (SOS 106), 1964. 546 pp., paper.

Gundlach, Bernard H., *The Laidlaw Glossary of Arithmetical Mathematical Terms.* Palo Alto, Calif.: Laidlaw Brother Publishers, 1961. 120 pp., paper.

Handel, S., *A Dictionary of Electronics.* Baltimore: Penguin Books, Inc. (R 19), 1962. 384 pp., paper.

Harriman, P. L., *Dictionary of Psychology.* New York: The Wisdom Library (Philosophical Library), 1947. 364 pp., paper.

Hough, John N., *Scientific Terminology.* New York: Rinehart Co., 1954. 231 pp.

National Radio Institute Teaching Staff, *Radio-Television Electronics Dictionary*. New York: John F. Rider Publisher, 1962. 190 pp., paper.

Spitz, Armand & Frank Gaynor, *Dictionary of Astronomy and Astronautics*. Totowa, N.J.: Littlefield, Adams & Co. (SOS 107), 1960. 439 pp., paper.

Tweney, C. F., & L. E. C. Hughes (eds.), *Chamber's Technical Dictionary*. New York: The Macmillan Company, 1961. 1028 pp.

Uvarov, E. B., and D. R. Chapman, *A Dictionary of Science*. Baltimore: Penguin Books (R 1), 1951. 240 pp., paper.

FOREIGN LANGUAGE DICTIONARIES

Andrews, E. A. (ed.), *Harper's Latin Dictionary*. New York: Harper & Brothers, 1880. 2019 pp.

Betteridge, Harold T. (ed.), *The New Cassell's German Dictionary*. New York: Funk & Wagnalls Co., 1962. 630 & 619 pp.

The Classic Greek Dictionary. Chicago: Follett Publishing Co., 1962. 835 & 262 pp.

Deak, Etienne & Simone, *A Dictionary of Colorful French Slanguage and Colloquialisms*. New York: E. P. Dutton & Co. (Dutton Paperback D 87), 1961. 210 pp., paper.

Gerrard, A. Bryson, & Jose de Heras Heras, *Cassell's Beyond the Dictionary in Spanish*. New York: Funk & Wagnalls Company, Inc., 1964. 160 pp.

Girard, Denis (ed.), *The New Cassell's French Dictionary*. New York: Funk & Wagnalls Co., Inc., 1962. 762 & 655 pp.

Glendening, P. J. T., *Cassell's Beyond the Dictionary in Italian*. New York: Funk & Wagnalls Co., Inc., 1964. 159 pp.

Klatt, E., & G. Golze, *Langenscheidt's German-English English-German Dictionary*. New York: Pocket Books, Inc. (GC 7), 1954. 526 pp., paper.

Larousse's French-English English-French Dictionary. New York: Pocket Books, Inc. (GC 24), 1960. 256 & 260 pp., paper.

Liddell, Henry George, & Robert Scott, *A Greek-English Lexicon*. New York: Harper & Brothers, 1868. 1705 pp.

Monadori's Pocket Italian-English English-Italian Dictionary. New York: Pocket Books, Inc. (GC 47), 1960. 271 & 305 pp., paper.

Peers, Edgar A., Jose V. Barragan, Francesco A. Vinzals, and Jorge A. Mora (eds.), *Cassell's Spanish Dictionary*. New York: Funk & Wagnalls Co., Inc., 1960. xvi & 1477 pp.

Rebora, Piero (ed.), *Cassell's Italian Dictionary*. New York: Funk
    & Wagnalls Co., Inc., 1964. xxi & 1096 pp.

Simpson, D. P. (ed.), *Cassell's New Compact Latin-English
    English-Latin Dictionary*. New York: Funk & Wagnalls Co.,
    Inc., 1963. 379 pp.

———————— (ed.), *Cassell's New Latin Dictionary*. New York:
    Funk & Wagnalls Co., Inc., 1959. xviii & 883 pp.

*The University of Chicago Spanish-English English-Spanish Dic-
    tionary*. New York: Pocket Books, Inc. (C 122), 1960. 226
    & 252 pp., paper.

SPECIALIZED DICTIONARIES

Abrams, M. H., *A Glossary of Literary Terms*. New York: Holt,
    Rinehart & Winston, 1964. 105 pp., paper.

American Geological Institute, *Dictionary of Geological Terms*.
    Garden City, New York: Doubleday & Co., Inc. (Dolphin
    C 360), 1962. 545 pp., paper.

Andrews, Wayne (ed.), *Concise Dictionary of American History*.
    New York: Charles Scribner's Sons, 1962. 1156 pp.

Barnet, Sylvan, Morton Berman, and William Burto, *A Dictionary
    of Literary Terms*. Boston: Little, Brown & Co., 1960. 96
    pp., paper.

Bierce, Ambrose, *The Devil's Dictionary*. New York: Dover Pub-
    lications Inc., 1958. 145 pp., paper.

Burgess, F. H., *A Dictionary of Sailing*. Baltimore: Penguin Books,
    Inc. (R 18), 1961. 237 pp., paper.

Cohen, J. M., and M. J. Cohen, *The Penguin Dictionary of Quota-
    tions*. Baltimore: Penguin Books, Inc. (R 16), 1963. 664
    pp., paper.

Colby, Frank O., *University Pronouncing Dictionary of Trouble-
    some Words*. New York: Thomas Y. Crowell Co. (Apollo
    A 94), 1964. 399 pp., paper.

Devlin, Joseph, *A Dictionary of Snyonyms and Antonyms*. New
    York: Popular Library, Inc. (W 1107), 1961. 384 pp.,
    paper.

Elliott, Florence, and Michael Summerskill, *A Dictionary o
    Politics*. Baltimore: Penguin Books (R 10), 1964. 396 pp.,
    paper.

Evans, Bergen, and Cornelia Evans, *A Dictionary of Contemporar
    American Usage*. New York: Random House, 1957. 567 pp

Ewen, David, *Encyclopedia of Concert Music*. New York: Hill &
    Wang, 1959. 566 pp.

————————, *Encyclopedia of the Opera*. New York: Hill &
    Wang, 1963. 594 pp.

Fowler, H. W., *A Dictionary of Modern English Usage*. Oxford: Clarendon Press, 1961. 742 pp.

Freeman, John (ed.), *Brewer's Dictionary of Phrase and Fable*. New York: Harper & Row, 1963. 970 pp.

Goldin, Hyman E., et al., *Dictionary of American Underworld Lingo*. New York: The Citadel Press (C 113), 1962. 327 pp., paper.

Gregg, John R., et al., *Gregg Shorthand Dictionary*. New York: McGraw-Hill, 1963. 376 pp.

Hastings, James (ed.), *Dictionary of the Bible,* revised edition. New York: Charles Scribner's Sons, 1963. 1059 pp.

Hopkins, Joseph G. E. (ed.), *Concise Dictionary of American Biography*. New York: Charles Scribner's Sons, 1964. 1273 pp.

Jacobs, Arthur, *A New Dictionary of Music*. Baltimore: Penguin Books, Inc. (R 12), 1963. 416 pp., paper.

Johnson, Burges, *New Rhyming Dictionary and Poet's Handbook,* revised edition. New York: Harper & Row, Publishers, Inc., 1957. 464 pp.

Jordan, Joseph, *A Handbook for Terrible Spellers, the backwords dictionary*. New York: Innovation Press (331 Madison Ave.), 1964. 44 pp., paper.

Kirkwood, G. M., *A Short Guide to Classical Mythology*. New York: Holt, Rinehart and Winston, 1959. 109 pp., paper.

Kling, Samuel G., *The Legal Encyclopedia for Home and Business*. New York: Permabooks (M 5012), 1959. 565 pp., paper.

Levinson, Leonard Louis, *The Left Handed Dictionary*. New York: Collier Books (AS 495), 1963. 254 pp., paper.

Lewis, Norman, *Comprehensive Word Guide to the English Language*. Garden City, N.Y.: Doubleday & Co., Inc., 1958. 912 pp.

Mawson, C. O. Sylvester, *Dictionary of Foreign Terms*. New York: Bantam Books (NR 35), 1961. 335 pp., paper.

Mayberry, George, *A Concise Dictionary of Abbreviations*. New York: Tudor Publishing Co., 1961. 159 pp.

McAdam, E. L., Jr., and George Milne, *Johnson's Dictionary, a modern selection*. New York: Pantheon Books (Random House), 1963. 465 pp.

Moore, W. G., *A Dictionary of Geography*. Baltimore: Penguin Books (R 2), 1963. 196 pp., paper.

Murray, Peter, and Linda Murray, *A Dictionary of Art and Artists*. Baltimore: Penguin Books, Inc. (R 14), 1959. 355 pp., paper.

Nevins, Albert J., M. M. (ed.), *The Maryknoll Catholic Diction-*

ary. New York: Dimension Books (Grosset & Dunlap), 1965. 710 pp.

Newmark, Maxim, *Dictionary of Foreign Words.* Totowa, N.J.: Littlefield, Adams & Co. (SOS 142), 1962. 245 pp., paper.

The Oxford Dictionary of Quotations, 2nd edition. New York: Oxford University Press, 1955. 1003 pp.

Partridge, Eric, *A Dictionary of Cliches.* New York: E. P. Dutton & Co. (D 128), 1963. 259 pp., paper.

—————————, *A Dictionary of Slang and Unconventional English.* New York: Macmillan.

—————————, *Shakespeare's Bawdy.* New York: E. P. Dutton & Co. (D 55), 1960. 226 pp.

Prochnow, Herbert, *A Dictionary of Wit, Wisdom and Satire.* New York: Harper & Row, Publishers, Inc., 1962. 243 pp.

Roget's International Thesaurus, 3rd edition. New York: Thomas Y. Crowell Co., 1962. 1258 pp.

Schwartz, Robert J., *The Complete Dictionary of Abbreviations.* New York: Thomas Y. Crowell Co., 1959. 211 pp.

Seyffert, Oskar, *Dictionary of Classical Antiquities.* New York: Meridian Books, Inc. (ML 2) 1960. 716 pp., paper.

Shipley, Joseph T., *Dictionary of Early English.* Totowa, N.J.: Littlefield, Adams & Co. (SOS 150), 1963. 753 pp., paper.

Smith, Sir William, *Smaller Classical Dictionary.* New York: E. P. Dutton & Co. (D 12), 1958. 319 pp., paper.

Soule, Richard, *Soule's Dictionary of English Synonyms.* New York: Bantam Books (NR 9), 1961. 528 pp., paper.

Webster's Biographical Dictionary. Springfield, Mass.: G. & C. Merriam Co., 1962. 1698 pp.

Webster's Dictionary of Synonyms. Springfield, Mass.: G. & C. Merriam Co., 1951. 907 pp.

Webster's Geographical Dictionary. Springfield, Mass.: G. & C. Merriam Co., 1962. 1293 pp.

Wentworth, Harold, and Stuart Berg Flexner, *Dictionary of American Slang.* New York: Thomas Y. Crowell Co., 1960. 669 pp.

Zimmerman, John E., *Dictionary of Classical Mythology.* New York: Harper & Row, 1964. 256 pp.

BOOKS ABOUT PROPER NAMES

Ames, Winthrop, *What Shall we Name the Baby?* New York: Simon & Schuster, 1963. 187 pp., paper.

Foreign Versions of English Names. Washington, D.C.: U.S. Govt. Printing Office (M 131, 30c), 1962. Paper.

Gudde, Erwin G., *California Place Names*. Berkeley, California: University of California Press, 1962. 383 pp.

Patridge, Eric, *Name This Child, a dictionary of given or Christian names*. London: Hamish Hamilton, 1963. 126 pp.

Pei, Mario, and Eloise Lambert, *The Book of Place Names*. New York: Lothrop, Lee & Shepard Co., 1961. 178 pp.

Rule, Lareina, *Name Your Baby*. New York: Bantam Books (SR 40), 1963. 210 pp.

Sanchez, Nellie Van de Grift, *Spanish and Indian Place Names of California*. San Francisco: A. M. Robertson, 1922. 454 pp.

Smith, Elsdon C., *Dictionary of American Family Names*. New York: Harper & Brothers, 1956. 244 pp.

Stewart, George R., *Names on the Land*. Boston: Houghton-Miflin, 1958.

BOOKS ABOUT WORDS

Adams, J. Donald, *The Magic and Mystery of Words*. New York: Holt, Rinehart & Winston, 1963. 117 pp.

Brown, Ivor, *A Word in Your Ear,* and *Just Another Word*. New York: E. P. Dutton & Co., 1945. 136 & 128 pp.

Evans, Bergen, *Comfortable Words*. New York: Random House, 1962. 379 pp.

Funk, Charles Earle, *Heavens to Betsy! and other curious sayings*. New York: Harper & Row, 1955. 224 pp.

——————, *A Hog on Ice and other curious expressions*. New York: Harper & Row, 1948. 214 pp.

——————, and Charles Earle Funk, Jr., *Horsefeathers and other curious words*. New York: Harper & Row, 1958. 240 pp.

——————, *Thereby Hangs a Tale, stories of curious word origins*. New York: Harper & Row, 1950. 303 pp.

Funk, Wilfred, *Word Origins and Their Romantic Stories*. New York: Grosset & Dunlap, 1950. 432 pp.

Gardner, Martin (ed.), *Oddities and Curiosities of Words and Literature,* by C. C. Bombaugh. New York: Dover Publications, Inc. (T 759), 1961. 375 pp., paper.

Greenough, James B., and George Lyman Kittredge, *Words and Their Ways in English Speech*. New York: Macmillan Paperbacks (MP 65), 1961. 431 pp., paper.

Hixson, Jerome C., and I. Colodny, *Word Ways, a study of our living language*. New York: American Book Company, 1939. 338 pp.

Levitt, John, and Joan Levitt, *The Spell of Words*. New York: The Philosophical Library, 1959. 224 pp.

Lewis, C. S., *Studies in Words*. Cambridge: University Press, 1961. 240 pp.

Lewis, Norman, *New Power with Words*. New York: Thomas Y. Crowell, 1964. 326 pp.

——————, *Word Power Made Easy*. New York: Permabooks (M 4020), 1955. 457 pp., paper.

Mathews, Mitford M., *American Words*. New York: World Publishing Co., 1959. 246 pp.

Moore, John, *You English Words*. New York: J. B. Lippincott Co., 1962. 254 pp.

Morris, William, and Mary Morris, *Dictionary of Word and Phrase Origins*. New York: Harper & Row, 1962. 376 pp.

Nurnberg, Maxwell, and Morris Rosenblum, *How to Build a Better Vocabulary*. New York: Popular Library (SP 114), 1961. 382 pp., paper.

Partridge, Eric, *Adventuring Among Words*. New York: Oxford University Press, 1961. 72 pp.

Pei, Mario, *The Families of Words*. New York: Harper & Brothers, 1962. 288 pp.

Picturesque Word Origins. Springfield, Mass.: G. & C. Merriam Co., 1933. 134 pp.

Pyles, Thomas, *Words and Ways of American English*. New York: Random House, 1952. 310 pp., paper.

Radford, Edwin, *Unusual Words*. New York: Philosophical Library, 1946. 318 pp.

Wedeck, Harry E., *Short Dictionary of Classical Word Origins*. New York: Philosophical Library, 1957. 85 pp.

Weekley, Ernest, *The Romance of Words*. New York: Dover Publications, Inc., 1961. 175 pp., paper.

Wolverton, Robert E., *Classical Elements in English Words*. Totowa, N.J.: Littlefield, Adams & Co., 1965. 85 pp., paper.

BOOKS ABOUT LANGUAGE

Alexander, Henry, *The Story of Our Language*. Garden City, N.Y. Dolphin Books (C 383), Doubleday & Co., 1962. 240 pp.

Bloomfield, Leonard, *Language*. New York: Holt, Rinehart and Winston, Inc., 1933.

Bloomfield, Morton W., and Leonard D. Newmark, *A Linguistic Introduction to the History of English*. New York: Alfred A. Knopf, Publisher, 1963. 416 pp.

Brook, G. L., *A History of the English Language*. New York

W. W. Norton & Co., 1958. 224 pp., paper.

Chase, Stuart, *The Tyranny of Words*. New York: Harcourt, Brace & Co., 1938. 396 pp.

Cleator, P. E., *Lost Languages*. New York: New American Library (Mentor MT 427), 1959. 192 pp., paper.

Gleason, H. A., *An Introduction to Descriptive Linguistics*. New York: Holt, Rinehart & Winston, 1961. viii & 503 pp.

Hall, Robert A., *Linguistics and Your Language*. Garden City, N.Y.: Doubleday & Co. (Anchor Books A 201), 1960. 265 pp., paper.

Hogben, Lancelot, *The Mother Tongue*. New York: W. W. Norton, 1965. 294 pp.

Hughes, John P., *The Science of Language, an introduction to linguistics*. New York: Random House, 1962. 305 pp.

Jesperson, Otto, *Growth and Structure of the English Language*. Garden City, N.Y.: Doubleday Anchor Books (A 46), 1905. 274 pp., paper.

——————, *Language, Its Nature, Development and Origin*. New York: W. W. Norton Co., 1964. 448 pp., paper.

Laird, Charlton, *The Miracle of Language*. New York: The World Publishing Co., 1953. 308 pp.

——————, *Thinking about Language*. New York: Holt, Rinehart & Winston, 1964. 75 pp., paper.

Laird, Helene, and Charlton Laird, *The Tree of Language*. New York: The World Publishing Company, 1957. 235 pp.

Marckwardt, Albert H., *Introduction to the English Language*. New York: Oxford University Press, 1951. 347 pp.

Mencken, H. L., *The American Language,* one volume abridged edition of the 4th edition and two supplements. New York: Alfred A. Knopf, 1963. 777 & cxxiv pp.

Muller, Siegfried H., *The World's Living Languages*. New York: Frederick Ungar Publishing Company, 1964. 212 pp.

Potter, Simeon, *Modern Linguistics*. New York: W. W. Norton & Co., 1964. 192 pp., paper.

——————, *Our Language*. Baltimore: Penguin Books (A 227), 1953. 202 pp., paper.

Pyles, Thomas, *The Origins and Development of The English Language*. New York: Harcourt, Brace & World, 1964. 388 pp.

Sapir, Edward, *Language: an introduction to the study of speech*. New York: Harcourt, Brace & World, 1949 (and Harvest Books, 1955).

Tauber, Abraham, *George Bernard Shaw on Language*. New York: Philosophical Library, 1963. 205 pp.

Work-Pages

ROOT	MEANING

EXAMPLES

ROOT	MEANING

EXAMPLES

ROOT	MEANING

EXAMPLES

ROOT	MEANING

EXAMPLES

Root	Meaning

EXAMPLES

Root	Meaning

EXAMPLES

Root	Meaning

EXAMPLES

ROOT	MEANING

EXAMPLES

ROOT	MEANING

EXAMPLES

ROOT	MEANING

EXAMPLES

Root	Meaning

EXAMPLES

ROOT	MEANING

EXAMPLES

ROOT	MEANING

EXAMPLES